Let Gigi Tchividjian share with you the lessons she's learned through her struggles. You, too, will discover:

- *How to be content with the life-style God has chosen for you*
- *The importance of spending time alone with God every day*
- *How to find and obey God's will—in both the big decisions and daily occurrences*
- *The "quietness of heart and mind" you need*

Gigi
Tchividjian A
Woman's
Quest for.
Serenity

FLEMING H. REVELL COMPANY
OLD TAPPAN, NEW JERSEY

Library of Congress Cataloging in Publication Data

Tchividjian, Gigi.
    A woman's quest for serenity.

      1. Christian life—1960–   2. Tchividjian,
Gigi.   I. Title.
BV4501.2.T34   248.4   80-25103
ISBN 0-8007-5102-7

TO Stephan, who loves me, encourages me, and accepts me as I am.

TO Stephan-Nelson, Berdjette, Basyle, Tullian, Aram, and Jerushah, who make this quest a delightful challenge.

TO my mother, Ruth, my mother-in-law, Charlotte, and my two grandmothers, who give me courage and by their loving examples fill this quest with joyful anticipation and hope.

Acknowledgments

To Sarah—who cleaned, cooked, washed, loved, encouraged—I owe a debt, for being all that I could not be and doing all that I could not do while working on this book. She was forced to practice serenity while I wrote about it.

To Anne Polli I owe the great debt of not only lovingly and patiently typing this manuscript, but of encouraging and challenging me onward. She is a dear friend, in whom I have observed much serenity.

To all of those who have encouraged me and have been so very patient, I bestow my very deepest gratitude.

Contents

To all who are weary . . .

> God bless and fortify them,
>   God hear when they entreat,
> The strong, courageous people
>   Too brave to own defeat.
>
> And Oh, God Bless and help them
>   God answer when they call,
> The tired, defeated people,
>   Who are not brave at all.

JANE MERCHANT

Foreword

Gigi,

Do you remember that summer in the south of France, when Stephan's father took us to his favorite restaurant—the little one built and run by one remarkable family?

There was the old grandmother, who had suffered much during the war, her daughter (who had married the famous French bicyclist whose career had been cut short by an accident), and the grandchildren. Working together, they transformed their little home into a restaurant.

It is a charming place: casual, homey, with unique, imaginative touches everywhere. The family pets, both dogs and cats (obviously well fed), greeted the guests and wandered wherever they pleased—sometimes right under your feet. The other farm animals would come down the hill just back of the restaurant—for it was their feeding time, too. The food was delicious and was all prepared and served by the family: the husband, limping slightly from the old injury, cordially greeting the guests, supervising the cooking of the meat on the open fires; the children, taking orders from the guests and serving; the wife, graciously overseeing everything.

One night we arrived early, and there, at a table in the first small dining room, sat the old grandmother. She was dressed all in black. Even her head was covered with a black shawl.

She could hear little, and her old eyes were dim. Her grand-daughter was sitting with her, and as we paused to chat with the daughter and pass on greetings to the old grandmother, who heard and understood little, we noticed that the grand-daughter was gently feeding the old grandmother. Life had gone full circle.

I have recalled that picture, as I have watched your father being fed by his children. (Me, also!) True, he is not as old as the grandmother and he can hear and speak and feed himself. But he gives out so much. I have seen him physically exhausted and spiritually depleted. And I have watched with awe and tender appreciation as his own children have fed him spiritually: a message, a story, a word of appreciation, a Bible study. . . .

And now once again, in this book, the scene is repeated. Thank you, dear.

Mother

Introduction
I'm Tired, Not Tame

It was our eldest son's confirmation. Much effort and secrecy had gone into the planning of this important day. My mother and father had decided to surprise him and fly in for this very meaningful occasion in the life of their oldest grandchild. In addition, our sixth child was only five weeks old, and she was due to have major surgery the following day. Needless to say, although very happy, I was a bit weary—both physically and emotionally. However, I tried to be as serene as possible, under the circumstances.

During the luncheon that followed the confirmation service, one of daddy's associates, who has known me since infancy and my days of terror, began, as he has on many other occasions, to thank Stephan for all that he has done for me.

"Oh, Stephan," he said, "thank you so much for all that you have done for Gigi. Since she married you, she has blossomed into such a lovely woman! You have done wonders with her. I just don't know how you have done it. It is just wonderful! She is such a wonderful mother; she has matured so. Boy, you are just terrific! Thank you so much!"

After listening to this for a few minutes and looking at me, sitting there holding child number six in my lap, trying to keep numbers four and five from destroying the restaurant and still enjoy this special day in the life of number one, another associate, who has also known me since I was a child, looked at his colleague and said, "Gigi is not tame; she is just plain tired."

Someone once said patience often gets the credit that belongs to fatigue. It was true, especially that day: I was tired! I am often tired, and doctors have assured me that is perfectly normal, with six children and a large home to run. But I often find myself more than just tired in body and mind; I find myself tired or weary in spirit.

Webster defines *weary* as, "Worn out in strength, endurance, vigor, or freshness." I'm sure everyone can identify with one or all of these words. He goes on to say, "having one's patience, tolerance, or pleasure exhausted." It almost sounds as if he is describing a mother, doesn't it?

Even though they are closely related, there is a distinct, though fine, line drawn between fatigue and weariness. Fatigue is caused by manual and menial labor, by external pressure and exertion. It's not only normal, but healthy, serving as a built-in safety valve. Even the Lord Jesus became fatigued.

On the other hand, weariness often comes from internal conflicts. For a Christian filled with the Holy Spirit, whose aim is to glorify God, weariness should not be the normal way of life. We read in John 15:8: "Herein is my Father glorified, that ye bear much fruit...." The definition of weariness is not very compatible with that of the fruit produced in the life of the believer who is longing to glorify God. We read in Galatians 5:22, 23 (AMPLIFIED) that the fruit produced by the Holy Spirit is "... love, joy (gladness), peace, patience (an even temper, forbearance), kindness, goodness (benevolence), faithfulness; (Meekness, humility) gentleness, self-control (self-restraint)...."

Looking back to my childhood, I can remember my mother and grandmothers being bone tired and fatigued, but seldom weary. They had learned the secret of living a life so in tune with the Spirit of the Lord that they were able to produce the fruit of the Spirit from within, even when worn out from without.

Satan, who thrives on attacking us when we are tired and down, didn't have much of an opportunity, with them. They lived lives characterized by inner quiet (even though they hollered at us from time to time), and the more I thought about it, the more I longed for this same serenity.

I had read in Jeremiah: "If you have raced with men on foot and they have worn you out, how can you compete with horses? If you stumble in safe country, how will you manage in the thickets. . . ?" (Jeremiah 12:5 NIV). If I become weary now, with all that I have—my health, a loving husband, six beautiful, healthy children, a lovely home, plenty of food to eat, freedom, and peace—what in the world would I be like if things got tough? I began to wonder and think about the things that caused weariness in my life. The causes of my fatigue were very obvious, but I had to search deeper, to find the causes of my weariness. I wanted to be prepared to run with horses and manage in the thickets.

One day, for fun, I decided to ask my four-year-old what some of the things were that made him weary. He thought a moment, and then he began to list some of them: running, waiting while I shopped, carrying big rocks, building houses, playing too much, climbing up big mountains. I discovered the things that caused weariness in a four-year-old were not that different from the things that caused his mother, thirty years older, to be weary: running around, being too busy, carrying heavy burdens, waiting for the Lord, being too occupied with my own wants and wishes, trying to build my home and my inner, spiritual life, and climbing out of the valleys and up the mountain.

Hence, I give to you just a sampling, a little of this and that, on weariness.

A Woman's Quest for Serenity

1
Trying Is Trying

Dear God,
let me soar in the face of the wind;
up—
up—
like the lark,
so poised and so sure,
through the cold
on the storm
with wings to endure.
Let the silver rain wash
all the dust from my wings,
let me soar
as he soars,
let me sing
as he sings;
let it lift me
all joyous
and carefree
and swift,
let it buffet
and drive me
but, God,
let it lift.

RUTH BELL GRAHAM

ONE SUNDAY not long ago, Stephan and I were sitting in the small Sunday-school class with which we had been meeting for some time. All of a sudden, one of the women looked up at me and said, "Well, you have it all together." I blushed, then looked at her as if she had two heads. I couldn't have been more taken aback, because I have always considered myself a struggler.

Nothing comes easy for me, especially being good or having it all together. I remember, as a child, awakening each morning to the sound of the birds singing or the katydids chirping, longing and hoping with all that was in me that I would be good that day. I would ask the Lord, first thing, to help me be good and not let me blow it. I would then proceed to do all that I knew to do, in order to help Him out. I would give Him my day, have a few moments with my Bible, then descend the stairs, hoping that this just might be the day I would get it all together.

Well, sometimes I would make it through breakfast, but, more likely, I wouldn't even make it that far. I would pick an argument, or someone or something would set my nerves on edge, and I would lose my temper. Or I would say the wrong thing or talk too much, and, as Lane Adams describes it, "that sick feeling in the pit of your stomach, a mixture of hot anger and bewilderment, [which] says that you have blown it again," would rush over me. I would become so discouraged that I would give up on that day completely.

I was a good little repenter, however (perhaps it was because I had so much practice), and I discovered early that failure isn't final, so I would try again the next day. But, as the months turned into years and this pattern continued, I became more and more discouraged. I began to question, "Why try?" It seemed that, for me at least, living the Christian life was one gigantic effort. I would read that the Lord loved a gentle and quiet spirit (see 1 Peter 3:4), and since this did anything but describe me, I didn't see how I was ever going to please Him. I looked with envy upon those who seemed to be Christlike without struggling so hard.

I would read about the fruit of the Spirit, and I would examine my life and see so little evidence of patience, long-suffering, gentleness, and so forth. Then I would read Amy Carmichael's words: "If I take offense easily, then I know nothing of Calvary love," or, "if people fret me and little ruffles set me on edge, then I know nothing of Calvary love," or, "if a sudden jar can cause me to speak an impatient, unloving word, then I know nothing of Calvary love. For a cup full of sweet water can not spill even one drop of bitter water."

I fell so far short of all that I thought was Christlike that I began to wonder if the Lord Jesus lived in me at all. Yet I knew I had given Him my life when I was four, and I had reaffirmed this many a time. Even so, I would often sit in church or attend a meeting or listen to the radio or TV and hear a sermon about how the Lord could change our lives, making us new creations. Then I would wish that I were not already saved, so that I could start over and become really converted. Maybe then I would see the dramatic change in my life that I so much longed for.

> I read verse after verse,
> I find
> I am supposed to have
> Rest,
> Peace,
> Gentleness,
> Quietness of heart and mind.
> I don't.
> I pray,
> thoughts stray
> every which way.

I cannot even say
how I really feel.
If I try,
it comes out wrong.
Oh, how I long
to be
what I am not.

GIGI TCHIVIDJIAN

I remember being so desperate once that I read all I could on living a victorious Christian life. I was sitting in my home in Switzerland, reading one of those beautifully written books that describe the kind of Christian life I longed to live. All of a sudden, the tears streamed down my face, and in utter frustration, I cried aloud, "But how? How? How do I do it?"

I had put an awful lot of effort into *trying:* trying to be good; trying to be the sister and daughter I thought I should be; trying to be kind to others; trying not to get nervous, even when my nerves were stretched thin; trying to be a patient mother; trying to be the loving wife Stephan needs; trying to be a good homemaker; trying to be a loyal friend, always ready to listen and be of help. I came to the very logical conclusion that trying is trying—and tiring.

Approximately a dozen years have come and gone since that day. Many more tears of frustration have found their way down my cheeks, and that was not to be the last time I would cry out, "But how?" I am still trying. I know now that I do not have it all together, but I have learned many things since that day, and I am so grateful that I never gave up in total despair.

Living With Goals

I like instant things. I love nurseries and hothouses. I can go in, and in a matter of minutes, I can acquire all the lovely, fragrant ingredients for an instantly beautiful, mature, full-grown garden. There is something rewarding about nurturing a seed and watching its growth, but that takes time, and since I am short on patience, that isn't for me. I love tennis, but I gave up after one set of lessons, because I couldn't play like the instructor. If I need to diet, I fast for a week, because I want to see instant results. All of a sudden, I began to see that I was doing the same thing in my spiritual life.

My husband, Stephan, is a psychologist, and he has patiently tried to teach my impatient soul and spirit something about goals: the importance of having goals, both long-term and short-term, and the importance of being able to differentiate between the two. I have plenty of goals—too many—but the mistake I continually make is taking one of these goals, which is or should be a long-term goal, and expecting to see immediate, short-term results. I do the same with jobs or projects. I want to see the results right away and have very little patience with the painstaking details that make the end result so rewarding.

I have little, if any, artistic ability. One of the reasons is that I lack the patience to wait for long-term results. I once thought it was time for me to take up some artistic project, so I decided to try decoupage. I went to the nearest art-supply store and gathered all the necessary material to keep me busy for weeks. I arrived home and immediately spread all of my wares out on the kitchen counters and began to become "artistic." All went well until I read that you have to let each coat of shellac dry before you can put on another one, and that a dozen or more coats of shellac were recommended.

That did it! I became impatient and tried to hurry the process along by adding the next coat before the first one was dry. The whole project was a fiasco, and I gave up on decoupage completely. Instead of accepting the short-term goal and being satisfied that the project was progressing nicely, I wanted to reach the long-term goal immediately.

So it has been in my spiritual growth. I get all excited and revved up after hearing a good message or reading a good book, and start trying to put into practice all I have heard or read. I make wonderful resolutions and set fantastic goals, but after a few weeks, if I do not see results, I become terribly discouraged and tend to give up altogether.

On Christmas or birthdays, my children sometimes receive articles of clothing that are too big. Their desire is to wear the clothing immediately, but when they put it on, it falls down around their legs or they just stand there and flop around in it, so it is placed in the drawer until they grow into it. Growing is a long-term process, which cannot be rushed.

So is spiritual fruit growing. There are no shortcuts to true spiritual maturity. In fact, my ultimate goal will not be realized until I see my Saviour face-to-face. ". . . I shall be satisfied, when I awake, with thy likeness" (Psalms 17:15).

Practicing Patience

Growing up in a small community inhabited mostly by retired missionaries and pastors and being raised in a Christian home, I was surrounded all through my childhood by beautiful examples of mature, full-grown, fragrant Christians. They had all been walking life's road hand in hand with their Lord for many years. Then I attended a Christian boarding school, where I was required to read many of the Christian classics of godly men and women who either didn't seem to have struggles in their Christian walk or were reluctant to share them, if they did. So I thought the word *Christian* was synonymous with "godly," "Christlike," "mature," "wise," "gentle," "perfect." It somehow escaped me, as a young Christian, that these dear saints had been walking with, working for, and getting to know their Lord for many, many years. It didn't occur to me that they, too, had struggled—some for many long, hard years. They had not been born full-grown or in full bloom. They had learned many lessons and had been taught much from their bumps and scrapes and spiritual skinned knees.

I remember once, as my two-year-old son was running to me, he tripped over himself and fell. He hopped up and said, "Oops. I dropped myself." He didn't get discouraged in his efforts to walk. He accepted this as par for the course, for someone of his age. He didn't compare himself to me; but on occasion, he did ask me to help him along.

Each time I "dropped myself" spiritually, the devil left his calling card of discouragement. I was measuring my spiritual growth and progress by the beautiful Christian role models that were around me. I was becoming more and more discouraged because I couldn't measure up, instead of simply accepting and acknowledging my limitations, as my little son had done, and asking for some help that would have been lovingly and readily given.

Amy Carmichael tells of watching a goldsmith in India refining gold. He patiently sat beside the pot, in a small cubicle. She asked, "When do you know when it is purified?"

"When I see my reflection in it," replied the goldsmith.

I failed to realize that these pure-as-gold saints had been through much refining and what I was observing was the reflection of the Master Goldsmith, after years of careful refining. I compared myself to them, as I compared myself to my tennis pro. They, too, were pros, but it had taken many years of growing, learning, trusting, submitting, abiding, obeying, and much practice. Since I was not (and still am not) a very patient person, I was extremely impatient with myself. I just could not understand why it was taking me so long to mature spiritually. I once heard a pastor say, "You are young only once, but you can be immature for a lifetime." I was sure this was to be my lot in life.

Struggling with this one day, I came across this little thought, by Pere Hyacinthe Besson:

> Be gentle, patient, humble and courteous to all, but especially be gentle and patient with yourself. I think that many of your troubles arise from an exaggerated anxiety, a secret impatience with your own faults; and this restlessness, when once it has got possession of your mind, is the cause of numberless trifling faults, which worry you, and go on adding to your burden until it becomes unbearable. I would have you honest in checking and correcting yourself, but at the same time patient under the consciousness of your frailty.

Over the years I have found that one of the greatest trials and miseries I have had to deal with is myself: my imperfections, my lack of self-control and self-confidence, and accepting myself, as the Lord has accepted me. I have tried so hard to "be good," to "get it all together," and I have failed so often that I have become quite discouraged. How grateful I have been for the patience of the Master Goldsmith, even with this poor metal.

Psalms 55:22 says, "Cast thy burden upon the Lord, and he shall sustain thee. . . ." Someone once said that *thee* is the greatest burden we have. For years I carried this burden around (and I still often pick it up again). I strove for victorious Christian living, and I spent much of my time in a heap.

The mother of a friend of mine once shared these thoughts:

> God loves and forgives me and accepts me, just the way I am, unconditionally. And He will love me into perfection.
> Because He loves and forgives and accepts me as I am, then I love (in the right way) and accept myself just the way I am ... in the body He has given me, with my limitations and imperfections—because He can use them as a showcase for His grace and glory.
>
> ELISABETH STRACHEN
> (now with her Lord)

I began to wake up to the realization that if I continued to try to live victoriously in my own strength, I could expect nothing but continued failure and discouragement. I began to see that I was expecting perfection. I was expecting more of myself than the Lord Jesus was expecting of me. I was trying to win this battle alone and was disappointed with myself when I lost. But the Lord doesn't expect us to fight alone. He says that He will go with us and fight for us. ". . . for the battle is not yours, but God's. . . . Ye shall not need to fight in this battle: set yourselves, stand ye still, and see the salvation of the Lord ..." (2 Chronicles 20:15, 17).

When I finally began to realize and accept this, I began to relax. Now when I fail (as I continue to do), I try to do as Brother Lawrence did, who was very "sensible of his faults, not discouraged by them. He confessed them to God, and when he had done so, he peacefully resumed his life."

Forgetting Yourself

Not only was I expecting too much and depending more on myself than on His strength, but I had fallen into the trap that Oswald Chambers refers to as morbid introspection.

I remember being so disturbed by my faults once that I began to keep a little journal. I thought putting them all on paper would perhaps help me recognize them and make me better able to deal with them. This little journal did reveal much, but not exactly what I had expected. Oh, the individual faults were there—the selfishness, the temper, the unkind words, the impatience—but the things that stood out from all the rest were the words *me, I, mine, my.* I was preoccupied with myself: with my faults, with how bad I was, how selfish I was, how impatient with the children, how grumpy, and so forth.

I was asked once to give a talk on Romans 6–8. In preparing for this talk, I was encouraged to discover that Paul, too, had fallen prey to morbid introspection. In chapter 6, Paul is exuberant. He is proclaiming the believer's freedom from the power of sin. Then, in chapter 7, the emphasis changes. He talks about the sin that indwells him, the problems that he has, doing what he should not do and not doing what he knows he should do. In chapter 8, he is again proclaiming the assurances of deliverance. It is of interest to note that in chapter 6, the emphasis is on Christ. In chapter 7, the emphasis is on Paul (the words *me, my, I* are found over forty times). In chapter 8, the emphasis is again on the Spirit of life in Christ Jesus.

When Paul looked at himself, he saw failures and strife. "Oh, wretched man that I am," he said. But when his eyes turned again to the Lord Jesus, he was able to speak of power, of deliverance, of victory. He closes chapter 8 with some of the most powerful verses in all of Scripture. He is able to proclaim with assurance, ". . . in all these things we are more than conquerors through him that loved us" (Romans 8:37).

There is such a thing as perfect forgetfulness of self. As George MacDonald said, "We remain such creeping Christians because we look at ourselves instead of Christ." There is most certainly a place for self-examination, but never for morbid introspection. When we examine ourselves before the Lord and He reveals to us our faults, our sins, our shortcomings, it is never to discourage us, because He also says, "If we confess our sins, he is faithful and just to forgive us our sins, and to cleanse us from all unrighteousness" (1 John 1:9). When He forgives, He chooses to forget.

I had read about mounting up with wings and living above all of our problems and shortcomings. I had read that, as a Christian, I should be as the butterfly, who flies high above the ground he once crawled as a caterpillar. Instead of realizing this was, or should be, a long-term goal, I became quite discouraged in my caterpillar state and looked with envy on all the beautiful, high-flying spiritual butterflies around me.

But, as I observed these "saints," these spiritual butterflies, I noticed they were not concerned about being saints at all; in fact, they were not even conscious of the fact that they were saints. They were deeply conscious of their need of and total dependency upon the Lord. They were much more concerned about their personal relationship and walk with the Lord than about their spiritual perfection or their usefulness to Him. They were so totally one with Him that all they did became a service to Him, whether it was washing dishes, caring for one another, or leading a Bible study. They did not spend time wondering if they had the Lord; they just made sure that He had them.

I began to see that the Christian life is not suddenly "mounting up with wings," but that it is *day-by-day faithfulness:* walking and not fainting; faithfulness in the little, everyday responsibilities and activities; doing "whatsoever we do, to the glory of God" (*see* 1 Corinthians 10:31); being faithful even when no one notices; glorifying God when there is no one to witness; being faithful in our everyday lives and circumstances, as they actually are.

In the cocoon, the caterpillar must have many doubts that he will ever be able to break out, much less fly. But one day he finds himself outside of his warm, safe cocoon, crawling around. Perhaps at times he even becomes a bit discouraged, as he observes a beautiful butterfly high above him, wondering if he will ever be able to fly like that. The days and weeks pass, and as he faithfully crawls about, without even being fully aware of what is happening, one day his wings take flight, and he soars high above the ground, where he once crawled. And I doubt that he is even aware that he has become a butterfly.

So it is with us. Becoming a butterfly is a long-term goal. But our crawling is packed full of short-term goals: daily, faithfully exercising faith, trust, and hope; being obedient; abiding in the living and written Word of God; never allowing Satan to snatch away our hope through discouragement and despair.

We have the promise that "... he which hath begun a good work in you will perform it until the day of Jesus Christ" (Philippians 1:6). In Psalms 138:8 we read, "The Lord will perfect that which concerneth me...." He has loved me too much to quit now. He has a personal interest in making sure that one day I "mount up with wings."

I have always had a battle with my temper. My toleration point seems so low, and my fuse so short. Someone once described a certain woman as "always being on the edge of a scream." Well, this pretty well described me. When I would get nervous or angry, I would say things I regretted the moment they were out.

One day, in discouragement and total frustration, I said, "Lord, I can't control my temper or my tongue, and I am tired and worn-out from trying. So I am going to quit trying and let You handle it."

I forgot about my prayer and went on about my day. Days passed into weeks, and weeks into months. Slowly I began to realize that things didn't seem to make me quite so uptight. In fact, it had been quite a while since I had lost my temper. I had "mounted up with wings," and I hadn't even noticed. I just bowed my head and humbly said, "Thank You." How important it is, when you fly, to fly humbly.

Possessing the Land

Samuel Rutherford once said, "The closer to heaven you get, the nearer hell you will feel." My eldest son was once quite discouraged in his Christian growth. He was concerned about the devil and how it often seemed the devil liked to pick on him. He expressed his concern to my mother one night when he was sleeping at her house. She thought for a moment, then she said something like this: "Stephan-Nelson, do you see that lovely African violet over there? The bugs have been pestering it to death. I have to constantly keep a watch on it. But do you see the beautiful arrangement of artificial flowers on the table there? Well, the bugs never bother those plastic, artificial flowers. The bugs only go after the real."

So it is with us, when we are pestered by Satan. We can take courage, because Satan, too, only goes after the real.

In Numbers 13, we read the story of the ten spies sent into the Promised Land to appraise it. When they returned, they reported all the obstacles, especially the giants who inhabited the land and the great, walled cities. They were discouraged and proceeded to discourage all the others. But Caleb, who had seen the same things, had faith in God and encouraged the people to go in and possess the land.

So it is with us. Satan spends his time pointing out all the giants and walled cities in our lives. Some of us allow Satan to preoccupy us with the problem, so we fail to possess the blessings of God with the power of God. Some see giants; others see God.

Henry Dubanville said, "We have been promised a safe arrival, but not a smooth voyage." The book of Deuteronomy gives us a beautiful picture of this voyage—a picture of possessing the land day by day, little by little. He is right there, to encourage and help and even bear us up, when necessary. But there are conditions: obedience (simple obedience to His Word), the necessity of total dependence upon Him, and abiding in the Word.

Recently, my mother was asked what had been her secret to peace, as she left home (which was China) to go away to boarding school in Korea; then on to the United States, where she was for many years separated from her parents by thousands of miles; on through the doubts she encountered in college; then her marriage and life with Daddy, who was away much of the time, so that the rearing of the children became primarily her responsibility. How had she done it all and yet remained strong in her faith (and also gentle, sweet, and lots of fun to live with)?

Her reply was simple. As she picked up an old, childhood Bible that she had found tucked away, she said, "I was able because of the written and Living Word of God." From our earliest days, she instilled in us that same love and dependency on the Person of Jesus Christ and in His written Word, the Bible. She taught us to love it, to depend on it, to claim its promises, to memorize it.

Stephan and I have encouraged the same love for the Scriptures in our own children. We have tried to teach them, in practical ways, that they can always depend upon the Living Word of God as their source of real strength and encouragement in their day-to-day lives.

Not long ago, our oldest daughter was having a real battle with Satan. He began to whisper lies to her, until she became quite discouraged in her Christian walk. For example, he would try to persuade her that she was untruthful or dishonest, when in reality, she is extremely honest and truthful, with a very tender conscience.

Stephan and I did all we could to encourage her and to assure her that, since this torment was from Satan, she must not believe him. But although this helped, it did not bring the needed victory, and the battle continued for some time. All of a sudden, her load began to lift. We were so thrilled. One day I asked her what had changed. She told me she had taken the Bible verses and catechism passages she had put to memory and refuted Satan's lies with them. At an early age, she was learning the reality of the power and strength received from the Living Word.

We live in Florida, where field mice and cockroaches would take over, if given half a chance. We do our best to rid ourselves of these pests. The bug man comes once a month to spray and set numerous traps, and we work hard at keeping the crumbs that tempt these critters to a minimum. But, try as we will, it isn't long before I begin to notice the telltale signs in my drawers and cupboards.

There is one very interesting thing about these pests: They flee from the light. I attended a boarding school in central Florida, and I can still remember going into the big kitchen at night and flipping the switch and hearing much scurrying of little cockroach feet.

Once my mother told me about a time when she was worried and discouraged. She was so preoccupied with her concern that she awoke in the middle of the night and couldn't go back to sleep. So she arose, and, taking her Bible, she went into the other room and began to read. She said that as she began to absorb the light of His Living Word, all the cockroaches and mice of worry, discouragement, doubt, and despair quickly fled.

When we walk with the Lord
In the light of His Word,
What a glory He sheds on our way!

Not a shadow can rise,
Not a cloud in the skies,
But His smile quickly
drives it away.

JOHN H. SAMMIS

David said, "My soul cleaveth unto the dust: quicken thou me according to thy word" (Psalms 119:25). I once took this psalm and listed all that the Word of God is and all that it does. I was amazed.

It cleanses (v. 9). It keeps us from sin (v. 11). It revives (v. 25). It strengthens (v. 28). It saves (v. 41). It gives freedom (v. 45). It causes hope (v. 49). It gives comfort (v. 50). It lights our way (v. 105). What a source of encouragement! David knew this, and I have proven this to myself over and over again. His Word has never disappointed me or failed me—not once.

Living With Two Natures

However, I often disappoint Him. The other day I awoke to a nice, cool breeze—a welcome relief, here in southern Florida. It was also Sunday, so I had been able to sleep a bit later than usual, a welcome relief for a mother of six.

We ate breakfast and got ready for church with less panic and commotion than usual. By some miracle, we arrived on time, which relieved the entire church, since we sit in the front row, and it is very hard to slip in discreetly when you are ten in number.

Our pastor preached a wonderful sermon from 1 Corinthians 13, on the love of God. He asked us to substitute our own names for the word *love* in verses 4-7: "Love [Gigi] is very patient and kind, never jealous or envious, never boastful or proud, never haughty or selfish or rude. Love [Gigi] does not demand its own way. It [Gigi] is not irritable or touchy. It [Gigi] does not hold grudges and will hardly even notice when others do it wrong" (1 Corinthians 13:4, 5 LB).

Well, I knew this most certainly didn't describe this Gigi, but I was surprised at just how much I fell short of God's love once we left church and were riding in the car to meet the pastor and his family for lunch.

Our eldest son, who just turned sixteen, was learning to drive. I am sure I don't need to describe in detail all the emotions I felt about this, although he is quite a good driver. He asked his father if he could drive. Stephan agreed, asked me if I would sit in the backseat, and forbade me to say a word.

I tried; I really did. But I just couldn't help it. I didn't say much, just a little, anxious, motherly remark—just a helpful hint. Stephan said, "Shuu."

Again, just a little word or two escaped, a very small reminder: just a little remark from the back. This time, Stephan reminded me, gently but firmly, that I was to keep quiet.

Two people giving advice at the same time was too much for our son. My pride was hurt. I had already struck out in the area of being "very patient." Now I was into "pride" and "touchy." And to make matters worse, it didn't stop there.

A few miles down the road, Stephan said (perhaps to get my mind off the driver or to break the silence I was trying so desperately to keep), "By the way, honey, this may be the wrong time to mention it, but I opened the refrigerator this morning, and there are quite a few leftovers in it."

That did it! My pride was not only hurt, but I was just a little bit—almost—furious. So I replied coolly, "The kitchen, including the leftovers, is none of your affair!" Immediately, I was sorry I had opened my mouth. I thought back to the sermon and realized I had blown the whole thing. My "old nature" had just about ruined a perfectly lovely Lord's Day. How ashamed I was. I quickly said I was truly sorry, and because dear Stephan is further along in the school of the love of God than I am, he did not hold a grudge, but quickly and lovingly forgave me.

As Amy Carmichael said, "There is nothing better for our ease-loving souls than to be made thoroughly ashamed of ourselves." How true. I once again realized I couldn't do it alone. It had to be Jesus Christ, loving and living through me. His is the only name that can be substituted for the word *love.*

I have always been bothered by the fact that my old nature was still so obviously and noticeably there. I somehow thought that, once I accepted Christ, my old nature would automatically disappear.

Someone once said that an insight was a sudden glimpse of the obvious. One day I glimpsed the obvious. I heard a pastor explain that just because we have a new nature doesn't mean our old nature is gone. It just means that now we have to live with two natures, and the nature we feed will be the one to grow and prosper, while the other will eventually starve and shrivel up. How encouraging! There was nothing wrong with my having two natures, and I could be assured that, as I continued to feed the new nature and starve the old, the old would eventually die.

My mother has used this illustration to encourage me. If you go out into your yard in winter and look up at the trees, you will no doubt notice a few brown, dried-up leaves stubbornly clinging to the branches. Now, you don't take a ladder and climb up into that tree and pluck each old, dead leaf off. You wait. Springtime comes, and as the sap brings new life to that tree, the new leaves begin to appear, and the old, brown, dead leaves fall off quietly, all by themselves. No one even notices that they are falling off, until one day you go out and look up, and they are all gone, and instead, the lovely pale green leaves, pumping with new life, have replaced them.

So it is in our Christian walk. Concentrate on feeding the new life, and as the sap of the Holy Spirit flows through you, the old habits—the temper, the sharp tongue, the griping, the envy, and so forth—will fall off quietly, all by themselves.

I have discovered that, as I abide in Him and in His Word, I become more aware of His presence. Being fully conscious of the fact that He is there has been so helpful to me in "letting go and letting God," in being able to "mount up with wings." He really is beside me and cares about me, and as Bill Gaither so beautifully puts it, there is comfort and strength in just staying "layed back in His love."

As a child, I would sometimes go to bed a bit down or discouraged, or perhaps ashamed or sorry, and I would hold out my hand and ask the Lord to take it. I would then go to sleep in peace and comfort, accepting by faith that He was holding my hand tightly in His own.

Recently, a friend of mine was going through a very trying time. I asked her how she had quit worrying about it and continued on in real peace, in spite of the difficulty. She told me that being conscious that Jesus was right there with her, with His arms around her, gave her the needed peace and strength.

Often, I have sat with my hands palms up in an attitude of readiness to accept all of Him and all He had for me, just feeling His love and the freshness of His Spirit flowing around and through me. After a few moments of quiet, soaking up His love, I am renewed and refreshed and ready to "mount up."

In his book *How Come It's Taking Me So Long to Get Better?* Lane Adams tells about a conversation he once had with my daddy. "I was greatly burdened by my lack of spiritual progress, and I poured out my concerns to my friend. 'Billy, why am I making such slow progress toward the place I feel God would have me be in my Christian growth? Why does maturing take so long?' 'Lane,' he said, 'the important thing to know is that the only hope for either one of us is that the gap between our achievement and the perfection of our Savior is covered by the blood of Christ.' "

It is His completeness that makes up for our incompleteness, His perfection that covers our imperfections. "And ye are complete in him . . ." (Colossians 2:10). He is perfect, and until we see Him face-to-face, we will never be perfect, but one thing we can be, and that is real.

Discouragement is the devil's calling card, and if you have been trying and failing and trying again, if you have found trying both trying and tiring, don't despair. We may not be able to maintain a constant victory, and we may even become discouraged and defeated, but we should never go into permanent retreat. Frederick Temple sums it up this way:

This one thing we can give, and this is what He asks, hearts that shall never cease, from this day forward, to strive to be more like Him; to come nearer to Him, to root out from within us the sin that keeps us from Him. To such a battle, I call you in His name.

2

I Wonder If?

The two ways part now and I stand
    Uncertain and perplexed
    Whither, Lord, next?

One friend says this, another that
    I have no choice.
    Lord, for thy voice.

But look! one path is stained with blood.
    Footprints I see.
    I follow Thee.

RUTH BELL GRAHAM

I WONDER IF I should go to the grocery store today? I wonder if we should have chicken or roast tonight? I wonder if we should take a vacation this year? I wonder if I will get that promotion? I wonder if the kids will be happy with their new teachers? I wonder if I should start a Bible study? I must say this little phrase tens of times a week.

We are faced with hundreds of decisions each year, every year of our lives—some very small, insignificant ones, some large, life-changing ones—but they all tend to wear us down.

Each time I came home from shopping, I found I was totally exhausted. I couldn't understand why. I enjoy getting out and doing errands, I enjoy watching the people in the shopping centers, I enjoy finding a bargain; so why was I so terribly tired each time? After giving it some thought, I discovered it was all the decision making that wore me out. Should I buy this, or not? Which was the better buy, the nicer color? Would the next store have it a dollar cheaper?

So it is often, in our Christian walk and experience. We are faced with many everyday decisions with which we want to please the Lord. We also are often faced with very large, complex decisions with wide, long-range consequences, in which we seek and want the Lord's guidance and His perfect will.

Recently, Stephan and I were faced with a very big decision that would affect every area of our lives. Not only would it change the direction of Stephan's work, but it would mean a big geographic move involving a complete change in our life-style. We began to seek the Lord's will and wisdom. We could see many pros and cons, so we took paper and made a list, with all the cons on one side and all the pros on the other. We spent hours together, discussing all of the elements. We sought the advice of family and friends. We even asked the children their ideas. We prayed and fasted. We searched the Scriptures and talked some more. On top of this, we continued to carry on our everyday responsibilities. After a few days of this, we found ourselves totally exhausted. Then we stopped and asked ourselves if it was right to be so weary and tired and worn-out from seeking the will of the Lord.

Wanting God's Will

At the age of seventeen, I was faced with what was probably the biggest decision of my life. A man six years my senior, whom I didn't know well and hadn't even heard from in over two years, was asking me to marry him and move to Europe. Until that point, several significant decisions had been made in my life: whether I should go away to boarding school before I was thirteen, which college to attend at sixteen, which age I could begin dating, and so forth. My parents, after discussing and consulting with me, took the responsibility and burden of making these decisions for me.

Now, for the first time, our roles were reversed. After discussing and consulting with them, I was faced with making this momentous decision alone before the Lord. Needless to say, I spent much time in prayer, seeking the Lord's will, and I began to learn much. Even at that young age, I began to discover some principles of discerning the will of God. I began to discover some of the ways in which God leads and directs.

As I sat on the window seat, praying and looking out over the North Carolina mountains, I found myself asking some pretty difficult questions. I believed in God and acknowledged Him as Jehovah. But I began to wonder if He really cared about every detail of Gigi Graham's life. Did He really get actively involved in such things as our choice of a life's partner? Did it really make that much difference to God whom I chose? If He did care, what was His will? How did He want me to handle this important decision? I wondered if He would reveal to me His perfect will, and if He chose to do so, just how would He do it, and how would I discern it?

The first thing I had to know for sure was if I truly wanted God's will. You see, when I first opened the letter from Stephan, I somehow knew this was from God. I couldn't explain it; I didn't understand it; I didn't know why God had allowed it. But I had to understand what God's will was, concerning my answer. If I did say yes, it would completely change the course of my life. I would leave my family and friends and move to a strange country with a different culture. I would be surrounded by unfamiliar people, speaking a language that I neither spoke nor understood. I would be giving up my college education, and more significantly, I thought I was already in love with another man God had chosen for me.

So, I first had to be really honest and search my heart, to see if I was truly willing—willing, in a way, to start from scratch, to lay myself bare before the Lord, to give up much of what I held very dear, to step out in complete faith, putting my total confidence in Him.

I took my Bible and began to search the Scriptures. I found out that what I had been taught from childhood was true: He is concerned about the personal details of our daily lives and even has the hairs on our head numbered (*see* Matthew 6; 10). I also discovered He formed me in the womb (*see* Isaiah 44:24). But even more than that, He says, "Before I formed thee in the belly I knew thee; and before thou camest forth out of the womb I sanctified thee, and I ordained thee . . ." (Jeremiah 1:5). This meant that God not only made me, but He sanctified me—set me apart—and He had a plan for me. Jeremiah 29:11(NIV) says, " 'For I know the plans I have for you,' declares the Lord, 'plans to prosper you and not to harm you, plans to give you hope and a future.' "

Upon discovering these wonderful truths, my heart and my will had no other choice but to humbly bow before Him and say, "Thy will be done." When I knew that I wanted—more than anything else in the world—to do His will, to follow His leading, and to find His plan, I then made myself available to Him. This was the first step in finding His perfect will.

When He created us for His glory, He chose not to make us puppets on a string. He wanted us to have the freedom to choose to follow Him, the freedom to choose to do His will, to be available, to be obedient.

Being Available to God

True, I was willing. I wanted to do His will; but was I really available? I found out that to be willing was not enough. I also had to be available. I had to be accessible and usable. I had to be manageable and obedient. This was, and still is, a struggle for me. To be willing is a thing of the heart, and my heart is usually in the right place, but when I have to put some solid action into my willing attitude, it becomes another matter. The old self steps right in the way. Questions, thoughts, rationalizations, excuses—many things—begin to block my usability, my accessibility. It's fine to be willing, as long as I don't have to do anything about it—as long as the Lord doesn't ask me to prove my willingness and my availability to Him. So, after some honest self-examination, I took my awesome, wonderful freedom and told the Lord that I was not only willing, but I was totally available to Him. Through the years I have had to repeat this experience, as self creeps back into preeminence. I have to reexamine myself and once again make myself available to Him.

Day after day, as I sat overlooking the mountains, seeking God's perfect will, I discovered that in searching for His will, I could not rely on my feelings and my emotions. At every turn, my feelings and my emotions fooled me. I would awaken in the morning, after a good night's sleep, and I would feel strong and not only ready to say yes to Stephan, but ready to take on the world. The adjustments seemed minimal, the problems small; all the positive factors came into focus. My daddy would look at me at the breakfast table and say, "Well, Gigi, it looks like a beautiful Swiss morning this morning." (Since he had picked Stephan out for me several years before, he was a bit prejudiced.) But, after a hectic day, I would tumble into bed, and the tears would begin to fall onto my pillow, and I would say, "No, Lord, I just can't do it."

Have you ever noticed that when you are in a dark place, your feelings play tricks on you? Remember how it feels to walk through the woods at night, or through a parking lot, or even your own home, late at night in the dark?

Well, I was in the dark, as far as knowing the Lord's will, and my feelings were constantly tricking me. Once I realized this, I tried not to rely on them or take them too seriously, but this was not always easy. We women have a special sensitivity to our feelings and our emotions, which are very important. I believe the Lord can and does use them, but seeking and finding the Lord's will has to go deeper than emotions; it has to become conviction. Even though for a time I was in darkness and could not rely on my feelings, I could rely on the Lord. Micah 7:8 says, ". . . when I sit in darkness, the Lord shall be a light unto me." I didn't have the answer, but it was strengthening to know that He did and that He would reveal the answer to me in His time and in His way.

During those December days, as I longed for and sought His perfect will, I remembered a little illustration I had been taught as a young girl. There was a certain harbor that was quite treacherous and dangerous. In order for the captain to guide his ship safely into this harbor, he had to be very attentive to the three lights that were used to guide him. When all three lights lined up as one, he knew it was safe to proceed, and then and only then would he be able to bring his ship safely to port. As we seek guidance, we, too, have to be very attentive to three lights that are used to guide us into the harbor of His will: the Word of God, outward circumstances, and inner conviction. When all three of these lights line up, then we can proceed with assurance that we will be led safely into the harbor.

The Word of God

The Word of God is His principal means of guidance, and we can be assured He will never lead contrary to His Word. Sometimes He will lead us by the letter of the Word—very directly. For example, my younger brother had just become engaged and wanted me to go to North Carolina for a few days, to meet his girl. It was Easter week, and I was also needed at home. I began to pray and ask the Lord to give me an answer. I proceeded to make air reservations, but still had no direction, so I finally sat in a chair and told the Lord I was going to sit there until He gave me an answer. I took my Bible and continued reading where I had left off. After reading a few verses, I came across this one: "And the Lord said unto me, Arise, take thy journey ..." (Deuteronomy 10:11). To me, that was His direct answer. Everything else fell into place. The outward circumstances and the inner conviction all lined up with His Word, and so I packed and left. The children were cared for, and I had peace in my heart. However, this type of leading in my life is rare.

Although He can use the direct approach and speak through the letter of His Word, the Lord usually leads through the spirit of the Scriptures. As we read and meditate on His Word regularly, the Holy Spirit teaches us and enlightens and guides us. We cannot always take the Bible, open it, put our finger on a verse, and say that is God's leading. But we have many promises and assurances in His Word that He will and does lead us. Isaiah says: "And thine ears shall hear a word behind thee, saying, This is the way, walk ye in it . . ." (Isaiah 30:21). We are told in Psalms: "I will instruct thee and teach thee in the way which thou shalt go: I will guide thee with mine eye" (Psalms 32:8).

As I sat meditating on my window seat, I claimed His promises of guidance and direction. I listened for the voice behind me and found out that, in order to hear His still, small voice, I had to be quiet. "Be still, and know . . ." the Bible says (Psalms 46:10). ". . . in quietness and in confidence shall be your strength . . ." (Isaiah 30:15).

Both inward and outward quiet come hard for me. I am not a quiet person. I tend to worry and get agitated on the inside; on the outside, I would often rather talk to family and friends than spend time quietly with the Lord. I have a tendency to want to help the Lord out, rather than sitting quietly ". . . until thou know how the matter will fall . . ." (Ruth 3:18). First Thessalonians 4:11 tells us to study to be quiet. That takes discipline, and that in itself is hard for me.

I often get discouraged, because many years have passed since I sat there overlooking the mountains and learning about how the Lord guides us into His perfect will. And yet, it seems I still have so much to learn. I often sing to myself the words of a hymn:

> Speak, Lord, in the stillness,
> While I wait on Thee;
> Hush'd my heart to listen,
> In expectancy.

E. MAY GRIMES

In the matter of my marriage, I wished for a direct answer from His Word, but since there was no verse that read, "Gigi, get thee up and marry Stephan," He chose to lead me through the principles of His Word. I knew that the same Spirit says the same thing. I also knew Stephan loved and honored the Lord and that he had prayed much before he had written to me, asking me to marry him. I knew he would not have taken that step if he had not been sure of the leading of the Holy Spirit. So, if the Spirit had told him, wouldn't the same Spirit tell me? I also knew the Scriptures teach that the Lord is pleased when a family is of one accord. Since all of my family loved the Lord, I prayed that each one would be agreed on this matter. (And without exception they were, before we married.)

The Bible also teaches there is much wisdom in seeking counsel. Proverbs 13:10 says, ". . . with the well advised is wisdom," and in Proverbs 12:15 we read: ". . . he that hearkeneth unto counsel is wise." This didn't mean I ran all over, asking everyone I saw what they thought. This would only have brought confusion. But I knew a few people whom I looked up to and trusted, and I knew they, too, would seek the Lord's wisdom and guidance, so I took them into my confidence and asked their counsel.

There is definitely a place for spiritual authority. Sometimes it is misused or overdone, but in its God-given place, it is a blessing. It is also very wise and very helpful to know two or three persons to whom you can go for good, sound, balanced, spiritual counsel. So I sought counsel, I spent quiet times with the Lord in His Word, and I prayed much.

Outward Circumstances

The outward circumstances were difficult to understand, because there were just as many negative ones as positive ones. It was a stalemate. I knew I was not to lean on my own understanding, and yet the Lord gave me good common sense, and I knew He wanted me to use it. In most decisions I have had to make, my common sense was put to much use, but this was a bit different.

The Lord wanted me to learn an awful lot about trust, faith, and obedience. He wanted me to trust and obey. My common sense thought I was too young. The Lord knew that in order to make all the adjustments I would have to make, I needed to be young. My common sense told me the adjustments and changes would be too great, but the Lord knew I needed this challenge, to learn that He is all-sufficient. I thought it made much more sense to marry and settle close to home, but the Lord knew I needed to expand and broaden my heart and mind, in order to better serve Him. He knew (and my parents knew, too) that Stephan was just what I needed.

In later decisions, outward circumstances have played a much more obvious and direct role. For example, a few years ago, we moved back to the United States, and Stephan decided to go back to school, in order to get his Ph.D. We sought the Lord's direction and guidance, and when Stephan was accepted into a program at Marquette University, the outward circumstances were made quite clear: We were to move our family to Milwaukee, Wisconsin.

Outward circumstances can include many things, and when the Lord leads through these circumstances, it is often very common, very normal, very ordinary. Outward circumstances can include opportunities, needs, a transfer or job offer, physical needs, and so forth. Though God's leading is seldom extraordinary, it can be—and sometimes is.

But, it is usually through our daily, faithful walk that He lets us know what the next step is. I had a dear girl live with me and help me with the children. She stayed for two years, and after her second year, she believed the Lord was leading her to do something else. Her desire was to go back to school, so she laid her desire before the Lord and watched and waited for His leading. She knew that if it was His will for her to leave, He would open a door and show her clearly that she should walk through it. She also knew all open doors are not from the Lord, because Satan can open doors, too. So she told the Lord she was willing and available, she attuned her heart to His Word, and she waited to see how the matter (outward circumstances) would fall. The Lord tested her faith, and up until the last minute, she didn't know what He had for her.

Then the telephone rang. My paternal grandmother asked if this girl could come and live in her home, to keep her company, and in return, she would not only give her a salary and a home, but would pay for her schooling. How God honored this dear girl's faithfulness.

Other people, however, are always seeking God's will for their lives. They jump from one thing to another, run here and there, and consult with all their friends. They have yet to realize that God's will for them is to faithfully carry out their present responsibilities, faithfully doing the job He has already given them. I am confident that if He does have an alternate plan for their lives, He will show them, in a quiet, normal way, one day when they are least expecting it and when their present responsibilities are completed. God's will is often simply that we do the next thing, as it comes, as best we can and for His glory.

Stephan has a tendency to misplace things. When this happens, as it did recently with his passport, he gets frantic and goes through everything, looking for it. He looks in the most unusual places and leaves each place upturned. The more frantic he becomes, the more unusual the places become in which he looks, and the more confused the household looks. Later, when he has given up trying to find it and has become quieter, the missing object usually turns up in its normal place.

So it is with us, when we seek His will. The more frantic we become, the more confused everything becomes. It is when we give up trying so hard to find His will that He can show us—in the quietest, most ordinary, simple way—what He would have us do.

Often we are so preoccupied with seeking His will for ourselves that it becomes a very self-centered, selfish pursuit. We tend to close off and tune out others and their needs.

A godly pastor was once in a situation where he had to know God's guidance about a certain matter. While he was in his study seeking the Lord's will, a poor, sick widow sent for him. He reluctantly went to minister to this needy soul. While he was reading God's Word to her and praying with her, the answer he sought came to him.

Isaiah tells us, "and if you spend yourselves on behalf of the hungry and satisfy the needs of the oppressed, then your light will rise in the darkness, and your night will become like the noonday. The Lord will guide you always; he will satisfy your needs . . . and will strengthen your frame . . ." (Isaiah 58:10, 11 NIV). As we faithfully carry out our responsibilities and care for those around us and their needs, the Lord says He will give us the needed light and guide us and take care of us and strengthen us. What a glorious promise, especially for those of us who are wives and mothers. One of the surprising things about finding the will of God is that it is most often revealed in such ordinary ways, while attending to our daily responsibilities.

Inner Conviction

I find "inner conviction" is the most difficult part of discerning the perfect will of the Lord. Perhaps it is just the way I am made, or perhaps it is because, as a woman, my inner convictions are so closely tied to my feelings and my emotions. I will find myself sure of God's direction one minute, then doubting myself and His direction the next. I will be convinced of His leading in my life and take a step forward, only to take three steps backward. This, of course, is not the best or safest way to steer a ship, nor is it very pleasing to the Lord. We are not to waver. The Scriptures teach, ". . . he that wavereth is like a wave of the sea driven with the wind and tossed. For let not that man think that he shall receive any thing of the Lord" (James 1:6, 7). I listen and pay close attention to my feelings and my emotions, since they are God-given and are used of Him, but there comes a point where I have to let go in faith, with complete confidence in Him who is able to keep that which I have committed unto Him.

Sometimes we don't understand. Sometimes our mental or bodily reactions cause confusion. But we can have confidence that a loving, sovereign, heavenly Father will never lead His child astray and that His guidance is never unreasonable, although it sometimes is contrary to our human understanding.

The days passed, as I tried to decide if it was God's will I marry Stephan. I watched the shadows playing hide-and-seek over the mountains and listened to the preparations for Christmas below me, sorting out all I was learning and had learned. I was willing; I was available; I was ready to put action into my willingness and availability. I had sought the counsel of God's Word and my family. I knew that God would deal with the outward circumstances. My inner conviction, although fooling me at times, was becoming more and more sure of what God's will was for me. Although I had very little self-confidence, I had complete confidence in my heavenly Father. Now came obedience and taking a giant leap of faith. So, just before Christmas of 1962, a plane landed in Greenville, South Carolina, and a dear man emerged from that plane. I went to him, and with little romantic feeling or emotion—but with much faith and anticipation—I quietly told him the Lord had told me I could say yes.

My education concerning how God reveals His will did not stop that day. Stephan and I have had many decisions to make together since that time, including some very large ones, such as whether, with four children at home, he should leave business and go back to school. There have been smaller decisions, such as when and where to take a vacation.

We have found that God's principles for revealing His will have remained the same, but His methods are limitless. Sometimes He shows us His will immediately. Other times we must wait patiently for a long time. Sometimes He is very specific; other times He gives us freedom to make our own decisions, using our God-given knowledge and common sense. Sometimes He has led us through someone else. Sometimes He has hurried us along; other times He has said, "Wait" or, "Slow down." Sometimes He has tested our faith and trust. He has allowed blocks or closed doors at the last minute. Other times He has opened what seemed to be locked doors and straightened crooked paths. The truth of the matter is that, as my small son said, "God can do whatever *God* wants."

In Scripture, we see God using many unusual means to communicate His will and guide His people. He more often uses natural means, today. Elisabeth Elliot, in her book *A Slow and Certain Light*, says she feels "a little wistful now and then because God leaves so much up to us in discerning

His will." She says, "The exercise of the intelligence is taxing."

One of the Goodyear blimps is based near us, and it often flies overhead, flashing beautiful, colored, lighted messages. I have thought how wonderful it would be, if God would just use this blimp to reveal His will for me in brightly lighted messages. He might not use the Goodyear blimp, but He does reveal His will, in His way and in His time.

There are times when there are no easy answers and we are faced with very difficult, complex situations, in which it is extremely difficult to make a decision. We want the Lord's will more than anything else, but perhaps there are other people involved, who do not care about doing His will. Perhaps we are in a situation where we have to decide (to the best of our human ability) between the lesser of two evils. Perhaps we are faced with several bright opportunities, and we are finding it difficult to decide just which one the Lord would have us do. Perhaps our decision will affect many others, and so it has to be made unselfishly, abandoning our own desires and happiness. Perhaps we are faced with a situation that is tempting, but is not in the "paths of righteousness."

This is when I find strength and comfort in accepting by faith that He has the answer, even when I don't, and in knowing as a fact that *all* things somehow work together for good to those who love the Lord (*see* Romans 8:28). He promises in Isaiah that He will go before and make all the crooked places straight (*see* Isaiah 45:2). He also promises, in Isaiah 48:17 (NIV), ". . . I am the Lord your God, who teaches you what is best for you, who directs you in the way you should go." We have the assurance of His Word that He will lead us and show us His way.

Accepting God's Will

Dr. Edman, the late president of Wheaton College, put it this way:

> His guidance may be immediate and instantaneous, with deep assurance within and an open door before us. His direction may be delayed because other people are involved in His plan for us or the place of His choice is not yet ready. His leading may be by a Scripture that is plain and pertinent, or it may be by silence that is perplexing for the moment. Because He has a plan and a pathway far better than we can possibly imagine, He allows us to come to the complete end of ourselves and our best plans, and then He directs us hither to untrodden ways of sheer delight.

He has led me by all of the above ways, and it has been my experience that His way is far better than I could have imagined. But often it is not until some time later that I can see the "sheer delight" part of it. There have been times when it has been just plain hard to follow the Lord's leading, and sometimes we have to deliberately choose to follow His leading, even though it may be difficult. I know that He always has my best and His glory in mind, but sometimes my human, bodily, and mental reactions balk at His direction.

We were in Jacksonville, Florida—living one block off the beach and spending every possible hour in the surf and sand, soaking up the sun—when we got word that Stephan had been accepted at Marquette University, in Milwaukee, Wisconsin. When Stephan applied to graduate schools, I prayed that the Lord would not take us north of the Mason-Dixon line. I dislike cold weather, and I was unsure of the North. Well, the home the Lord gave us was in a town north of Milwaukee, as far as the freeway went, at that time. The excitement of the move and the purchase of our first home kept me going for a little while, but it wasn't long before my mind and body took on a complaining spirit.

The Wisconsin winter hit. I thought I was prepared for the worst. I was wrong. Thirty degrees below zero (with the wind-chill factor included, it was fifty-six degrees below zero) one block off Lake Michigan is pretty cold by any standards, much less those of a southern girl. I began to complain, like the Israelites in the wilderness, wondering why the Lord had brought me up there to die. Finally, I thought it was over. The middle of March arrived, and a decent day appeared. I came down with spring fever, so I called a nursery to see about planting trees. The woman laughed and asked how long I had lived there. Then she told me to call back in May. Sure enough, in April we had our biggest snowstorm.

Up until this point, there had been little sheer delight in our move. Whatever sheer delights the Lord was willing to give me were overshadowed by my bad attitude. I knew beyond a shadow of a doubt that the Lord had led us to Milwaukee. If that was true, then my attitude was truly a sin. I had to do some vital, healthy self-examination. I asked for forgiveness, and the sheer delights came in abundance. The cold weather didn't get better. In fact, over the years, the winters got longer and harder, but my attitude no longer hindered the blessings of God. Amy Carmichael has written a poem that has helped and blessed me on several occasions:

IN ACCEPTANCE LIETH PEACE

He said, "I will forget the dying faces;
The empty places,
They shall be filled again.
O voices moaning deep within me, cease."
But vain the word; vain, vain:
Not in forgetting lieth peace.

He said, "I will crowd action upon action,
The strife of faction
Shall stir me and sustain;
O tears that drown the fire of manhood cease."
But vain the word; vain, vain:
Not in endeavour lieth peace.
He said, "I will withdraw me and be quiet,
Why meddle in life's riot?
Shut be my door to pain.
Desire, thou dost befool me, thou shalt cease."
But vain the word; vain, vain:
Not in aloofness lieth peace.

He said, "I will submit; I am defeated.
God hath depleted
My life of its rich gain.
O futile murmurings, why will ye not cease?"
But vain the word; vain, vain:
Not in submission lieth peace.

He said, "I will accept the breaking sorrow
Which God tomorrow
Will to His son explain."
Then did the turmoil deep within him cease.
Not vain the word, not vain;
For in Acceptance lieth peace.

AMY CARMICHAEL

The writer of Hebrews says, "Lo, I come . . . to do thy will,
O God" (10:7). We are all here to do God's will. We were
created for this very thing, and the beauty of it is that He
cares enough about us to guide us and show us just what His
will is. He has a plan for each of His children, a plan as individual as each one of us, and He is longing to show us His
plan, His way, His will. Job 23:10 (AMPLIFIED) says, "But He

knows the way that I take [He has concern for it, appreciates and pays attention to it]. . . ." Our responsibility (and privilege) is to be willing and available, to totally entrust ourselves and our ways to Him. "Commit to the Lord whatever you do, and your plans will succeed" (Proverbs 16:3 NIV). Another translation has it, "Commit thy works unto the Lord, and He will cause thy thoughts to be agreeable to His will." Psalms 37:5 says, "Commit thy way unto the Lord; trust also in him; and he shall bring it to pass."

What a beautiful promise. There will be times we will be perplexed or bewildered, but we need never be worried. There will be times when great mountains will loom before us, but He promises to make a way: "And I will make all my mountains a way. . ." (Isaiah 49:11). When His guidance seems beyond our understanding or reason, we can have confidence that "His thoughts are not our thoughts, neither are His ways our ways, but His thoughts are higher than our thoughts, and His ways are higher than our ways" (*see* Isaiah 55:8, 9). When we do not have enough knowledge or understanding about a matter, we can say with Jeremiah, "O Lord, I know that the way of man is not in himself: it is not in man that walketh to direct his steps" (Jeremiah 10:23). But, we can claim the promise, "If any of you lack wisdom, let him ask of God, that giveth to all men liberally . . ." (James 1:5) and His promise of, "I will instruct thee and teach thee in the way which thou shalt go: I will guide thee with mine eye" (Psalms 32:8).

The closer we walk with the Lord, the easier it will be to discern His will. The closer we are to Him—the more intimate we become—the more our minds and hearts become like His. Hosea says, "Then shall we know, if we follow on to know the Lord . . ." (Hosea 6:3).

If we are really serious in our search for God's will, we can be assured that we shall know it. "If any man will to do his will, he shall know . . ." (John 7:17). Once we know His will, we have no option but—by faith and in His strength—to obey it, because the Scriptures tell us that when we know what to do and we don't do it, it is sin. Yes, it is a bit frightening, a bit risky. When we take our willing hearts and say, "Lord, I totally trust You. I deny myself and am totally available to You," and we really mean it, God will take us at our word.

He might even put us to the test, to see how sincere we really are. Until action is required, words and faith are easy. The action might just be doing the next task, serving others in some menial way, or it may require the giving up of something dear. It may mean adjustments, large and small; it may tax our emotions and our nerves. It may mean the simple act of being kind or patient, or it may mean simply relaxing, enjoying, and being grateful for all He has given us. But whatever it is, we can be assured of one thing: It will be worth it, and He will give us the strength to do it. "As for God, his way is perfect . . ." (2 Samuel 22:31).

Not long ago, I shared with a friend my concern about the unstable conditions in the world today and the uncertainty of the times in which we live. This friend replied, "The only safe place is the center of God's will." It is not only the safest place; it is also the most rewarding and the most satisfying place to be. As Mother Teresa of India said, "Holiness is doing God's will with a smile."

3

Too Busy?

OVERHEARD IN AN ORCHARD

Said the Robin to the Sparrow:
"I should really like to know
Why these anxious human beings
Rush about and worry so."

Said the Sparrow to the Robin:
"Friend, I think that it must be
That they have no heavenly Father
such as cares for you and me."

ELIZABETH CHENEY

THE ALARM RINGS about 6:30. I allow myself a few moments to adjust to the idea it is already morning, ask the Lord to bless my day, and pull myself out of bed (hoping the timer on the coffeepot was set correctly last night). I arrive in the kitchen, and immediately my day begins with a crescendo, whether I am ready or not. By the time I have closed the brown lunch bags; cooked the eggs just right (not too soft, not too hard), and tried to plan it so that they are hot, even if the teenagers are a bit late for breakfast; tried to force at least three bites of nourishment down the small ones; intervened in a couple of squabbles; reprimanded them for making so much noise they awoke the baby, when I had hoped she would sleep until I had at least one cup of coffee; and ushered them out to the bus, I am bushed. I already feel I have put in a whole day, and it is only 7:30. I have at least fourteen hours of busyness ahead of me.

Then, halfway through the day, someone may have the nerve to ask me, "And just what do you do to keep busy?" I am surprised and intrigued by this inquiry, because with all of my home responsibilities, it doesn't seem possible to do one more thing. I thought I was doing all I could possibly do and still keep my sanity, and yet I began to have guilt feelings every time I was not "busy." I remember several occasions when, upon hearing someone approach my front door, I felt terribly guilty if I was not in the process of doing something. I have even gone so far as to begin to bake a cake (from scratch, because it takes longer) when a repairman arrived, so I would be busy and he would not have the impression that I was a lazy housewife.

Pick up any ladies' magazine at the grocery store, and you will find umpteen more reasons to feel guilty: all those pictures of darling, homemade Christmas gifts that could save you so much money and give so much pleasure, if only you had the time and a little creativity; all those delicious, from-scratch recipes for your family, pictured in spotless kitchens where everything is color coordinated, including the cookie jar and the apron on the beautifully groomed woman. Turn a few pages, and you will read that in order to stay young and healthy and beautifully groomed, you need to fit a regular exercise program into your schedule. (A few articles do mention that carrying six loads of wash up and down the stairs, grocery shopping, pushing a vacuum cleaner, putting toddlers in and out of bed and bath is a form of exercise.) Continue turning the pages, and you will find a beauty routine, complete with leisurely bubble baths (it is usually my three toddlers who are taking the leisurely bubble bath at 5:00, not me), manicures, pedicures, diets, hair care, skin care, and so forth. Then you can read about all the job opportunities open for women, all the social needs women can and should get involved with, not to mention the PTA, the community, clubs, sports, and the church. This is all above and beyond the daily routine and responsibilities of running and caring for a home and family while being a loving, attentive, attractive wife and lover.

Where does it stop? There seems to be no end to the demands and expectations placed on women today. We are all plagued by time pressure. I am sure all of us have felt, at one time or another, that everything is coming in on us, that we are never finished, never caught up. The queen in *Alice in Wonderland* said, "It takes all the running you can do to stay in place. If you want to get someplace else, you must run twice as fast as that." How true this seems today. I sometimes find myself running, and if I take a moment to ask why, I can't find a good reason.

Being too busy has become a compulsion for many and a way of life for most. The effects of busyness are becoming more and more evident; in every area of our lives, the effects of being too busy are beginning to take their toll. How many of us suffer from tension, in one form or another? How many of us are difficult to live with because we are just plain overworked and overtired? We haven't learned, nor are we willing to learn or accept our limits. How many of us are so busy that we don't have the time to get really involved with the friend or neighbor who is hurting?

I have a hard time believing this kind of busyness is pleasing to the Lord, and yet, it is a battle I have to fight constantly. So often I find myself on the losing side of this battle, and I often become discouraged. How often I have been so busy that I have failed to encourage someone or forgotten to thank and praise a child for a job well-done or failed to take the time to be with someone who just needed a friend. How often I have been running around so much all day that I am too preoccupied to be attentive to my children when they arrive home from school or too tired to be loving to my husband when he comes home depleted.

> Nerves
> Tears
> Tensions
> Pressures
> Running all about
> It all builds up
> We can only take so much
> And then begin to doubt.
> We start to fall apart
> With a start,
> We begin to realize
> How we feel
> How we react.

We become afraid
We don't know ourselves
We find we lack
The strength and courage
We used to have.
We long for a new lease on life
But,
It doesn't come
Instead,
Inside strife
Continues.
We begin to reexamine.
We are all confused
We feel so unused.
So,
Tired,
Weary,
Eyes bleary
I ask
Why?

GIGI TCHIVIDJIAN

It is a battle, and I have come to believe it is a spiritual battle. Someone once said if the devil can't make you bad, he makes you busy. How true this is. But how do we handle this? How do we respond to all the needs? How do we answer all the requests? Are we to say yes each time we are asked to serve in some capacity? Are we to walk through every open door? The needs are so great, and there is no end to all we could be involved with: good, important, positive, helpful, spiritual activities we could be involved with. But where do we draw the line? Are we to just grin and bear it and go on until we collapse in a heap on the floor? I know many who equate busyness and activity with spirituality. The busier someone is, the more spiritual he appears, and it boosts his morale and feeds his ego to have someone ask, "How do you do it? How do you find the time and energy?"

Examining Priorities

But is this really pleasing to the Lord; is this what He really expects from us?

The Lord tells us, through the pen of Solomon in Proverbs 31:16 (AMPLIFIED), that the ideal woman "considers a new field before she buys or accepts it—expanding prudently [and not courting neglect of her present duties by assuming others]. With her savings [of time and strength] she plants fruitful vines in her vineyard."

Millie Dienert, a dear friend, once said, "Any activity we involve ourselves in that is not directly led by the Holy Spirit is just a bunch of busyness."

Here we are again, right back to the question of priorities. I am in a constant battle with my priorities. I think they are all in order, then I find that in a very short time, I have to work on them again. Being too busy is enemy number one to my priority list. I get talked into so many good things that are not among my priorities for this period of my life. One of the most difficult things for me is to say no to something or someone. And yet, I have found that when I lay that priority list, whether mental or written, before the Lord, I often have to say no in order to be obedient to Him.

In Ephesians 2:10 (NIV) we read, "For we are God's workmanship, created in Christ Jesus to do good works, which God prepared in advance for us to do." This means God has a plan for each of us. God has prepared an agenda for our lives. To me, this is so encouraging and thrilling: not only that God has a plan for me and for my life; but to know He cares so much for me that He prepared this plan in advance.

I also believe that if we abide daily in Him and in His Word and seek with all our hearts to do His will, then by faith we can rest assured that we are following His plan for our lives. How sad it would be, to get so busy and so involved in our own activities that we completely miss His plan for us.

The rush of other things tends to obscure His will and His values. This is why I have found it so important to examine my priorities—very honestly—before Him. It is not always easy to know what should be on my priority list, or in which order to place my priorities.

Not only do I examine them before Him, but I search His Word for advice and counsel. I also ask advice from my husband and family. Sometimes the counsel comes from a friend or a pastor, and sometimes it is given through the pages of a book that I am reading.

I remember once, when I was reexamining my list, that I was sitting in a doctor's office. I was reading a book on the Psalms, and I read Psalms 1:3: "And he shall be like a tree planted by the rivers of water, that bringeth forth his fruit in his season; his leaf also shall not wither; and whatsoever he doeth shall prosper."

There it was, right in front of me. With six children, it was obvious that my season, for now, was home, homemaking, mothering; that it was there that I would bring forth my fruit; there is where I would prosper. This verse also says the tree was planted by rivers of water, so I knew that, on top of the list, I had to put residing near the source. If I was to receive strength to bring forth good fruit and be productive in the home and prosper in my efforts, I had to abide in the One who said, ". . . If any man thirst, let him come unto me, and drink" (John 7:37).

I know that since my "season" is homemaking, the care of my family is to top my priority list. Right now, that occupies most of my time, but circumstances change, children grow up, responsibilities shift. With the children now in school most of the day, I have found I have a little more time for something else. This is where I have to consider carefully, before Him, any new field of interest or activity; I have to expand prudently and be careful not to neglect my present God-given responsibilities.

Imaginary Priorities

In making a priority list, I have discovered it is quite important to learn to discern between the demands, expectations, and responsibilities that are real and those that are imaginary.

For example, we have quite a large yard and live in an area where almost everyone has a lawn service. We do our own mowing and trimming, and I found I became quite overwrought and demanding about the yard. I was driving everyone nuts, especially my eldest son, who is our chief gardener. There is nothing wrong in working hard in the yard. It is good for me and for my children. There is nothing wrong with having a lovely yard. In fact, it would not be good stewardship to let it go and not care. But my motivation was becoming a bit confused. I do love and enjoy a lovely, manicured lawn, but I am afraid I was pushing so hard because each time I drove home, past all the lovely lawns with the lawn-service trucks out in front, I would feel badly that my yard didn't measure up. You see, I was beginning to put my yard and its beauty before my family. It got so bad that when we sat outside in the sun, enjoying one another, I would see a few weeds and comment that they should have been pulled. I couldn't enjoy my family or my yard. Now that was an imaginary demand.

I would do the same with my home. I would go to the home of a neighbor and see her home was clean and everything was in its place, and I would come home and go into a frenzy of cleaning and straightening. I wouldn't stop to think that she only had two children, both grown or in school, nor would I stop to realize she had probably just cleaned, knowing she was expecting guests. That was another imaginary demand. No one expects or cares if my home is always spotless, every toy picked up, every table shining like the wax commercials. What they do care about, what they do notice, is if there is warmth and love in the home. If I am honest, I have to admit that many of the expectations and demands are from no one but myself—not from my husband, not from my family, not from my friends, and certainly not from the Lord Jesus.

But as a wife, mother, friend, and Christian, I also have many expectations and demands that are very real and very necessary. It is not always easy to determine which ones are vital and which ones are not. Sometimes they even overlap, and I have not found an easy solution. I know I spend much of my day saying, "I have to," "I must," or "I don't have time," and I blame my being too busy on anything or anyone but myself. Often, it is true that I have to, because if I don't do it, nobody will. But sometimes (more often than I like to admit), I am too busy because I have chosen to be too busy.

A few years ago, I had a maid come to my home once a week to clean. The day she came, I would hurry with breakfast, so I could clean the kitchen and straighten the house before she arrived. She couldn't see it in such a mess! That is a perfect example of an imaginary, unnecessary (and stupid) demand that I put on myself and chose to do.

Urgent or Important?

The Lord has given each of us the ability and the freedom to use the little word *no*. I heard of a Bible teacher in my area who knew her women were all overcommitted and had them practice saying no. She told them to simply place their tongues on the roofs of their mouths and say, "No." Thomas a Kempis said, "It is thy duty, oftentimes, to do what thou wouldst not; thy duty too, to leave undone what thou wouldst do."

Making a priority list involves making conscious decisions about what we want to do, what we should do and are able to do, and what we should leave undone or are unable to do. Many of the demands on us are circumstantial and have to be dealt with accordingly. If we have a job, we have to show up at a certain hour and put in so much time and effort. As a wife and mother, I must see to the physical, emotional, and spiritual well-being of my family. And a basic fact is that caring for a family, especially with small children, takes time.

It takes time to plan and prepare meals; it takes time to bathe and entertain small folk; it takes time to be the peacemaker in squabbles; to discipline; to take an active part in the interests of the older children; to pick up dozens of toys several times a day; to keep the house decently in order. It takes time to be an attractive wife and to remain the desirable sweetheart your husband married. There are many books and articles written that give us valuable tips and shortcuts, but the fact remains that all of this takes time and energy, and there is just so much time in a day and so much energy in each one of us. Also, we must allow for our personal abilities and limitations.

It is just as important to know what our gifts are *not* as to know what they are. Each one is different, and the Lord has given to each one different gifts and different physical and emotional limitations. But He has given all of us the same capability of faithfulness, and that is all He requires of us: faithfulness. Each one of us is to be faithful, and that is why it is so important to take our list of priorities to Him.

It is difficult for me to believe the Lord wants us to rush around as much as we do, for the Lord is the author of peace, quiet, and rest. Dr. Charles Hummel has written a wonderful little booklet on this very subject, titled *Tyranny of the Urgent*. He suggests that even if we had more hours in the day, our problems would only increase, instead of decrease.

We live in constant tension between the urgent and the important. The problem is that the important task rarely must be done today, or even this week. Extra hours of prayer and Bible study, a visit with that non-Christian friend (reading that book to your child, taking a walk with that teenager, listening to your child's long, drawnout, detailed story, showing love and understanding to the tired husband) all these can wait.

But, the urgent tasks call for instant action, endless demands that pressure every hour every day. The momentary appeal of these tasks seems irresistible and important, and they devour our energy. But, in the light of time's perspective, their deceptive prominence fades; with a sense of loss we recall the important tasks pushed aside. We realize we have become slaves to the tyranny of the urgent.

Dr. Hummel goes on to remind us that, on the night before Jesus died, He said to His Father, ". . . I have finished the work which thou gavest me to do" (John 17:4). Jesus had not healed all the sick. He had not met everyone's needs. He had not raised all the dead or fed all the hungry. With much still left to be done, Jesus experienced peace and satisfaction that He had been faithful and had accomplished all His Father had wanted Him to do.

The Bible teaches that Jesus was tempted in all points, just as we are, and we know by reading the Gospels that He was tempted by busyness. He was pressured from every side. The demands of His family, His friends, and the crowds were never ending. He, too, experienced exhaustion. He, too, experienced the need to be alone, to get away for a little while. And yet, I do not get the picture of Jesus running about in six directions at the same time, but one of a steady pace, with His priorities under the direction of the Father. He was in constant fellowship with His Father. We read often how He went out alone to pray and spend time alone with God. If Jesus knew the importance of this and felt a need for this, how much more we need to be aware of the importance of spending time with the Lord. We need to be so careful not to be hurried out of, or "busyed out of," our relationship with Him.

My maternal grandfather was a very busy man. He was a missionary, medical doctor, writer, active church layman, father, and husband. But he always seemed to accomplish all he had to do and still have time to relax and to laugh, to read a good mystery story, play a game, or talk with family and friends. As a child, I often stayed overnight at his home, and without fail, when I would come down for breakfast every morning, I would see him in the living room, either reading his Bible or on his knees in front of the big rocker. I have a little sign in my room that reads, "If your day is hemmed in prayer, it is less likely to come unraveled." My grandfather proved this to be true.

One day Jesus went to visit His friends Mary and Martha. Martha, like any good hostess, was doing all she could to prepare for her guest. She was very busy, doing all the work (some real and necessary, perhaps some to make an impression or to be accepted). Mary, on the other hand, had been spending all of her time at Jesus' feet, and Martha wanted some help in the kitchen. She told Jesus to tell Mary to come and help her, and instead of telling Mary to go help,

He told Martha to take a "Jesus break." What Martha was doing was good, and someone had to do it, but Jesus was reminding her that the urgent could wait. He knew Martha was putting too much emphasis and importance on the cooking and cleaning, and not enough on being with Him.

I can identify so well with this story. How often the Lord has to remind me of the same thing. I used to think that perhaps He didn't really understand that, as a mother and homemaker, I had to keep up. I had to keep going, or I would never catch up. If I didn't do it, who would? I was, and still am, being deceived by this urgency.

Yes, all this work is important, in its place, but it is also terribly important to remember to do each day's work for Jesus with eternity's values in view. Jesus was teaching Martha something Mary had already learned: Eternity's values are far more important.

When we get too busy, not only the physical suffers, but the spiritual, the eternal. Of one thing we can be assured: It is not the Lord who loads us down until we break, or get an ulcer, or suffer a heart attack, or divide our family, or turn our kids off. He says, "Come unto me, all ye that labour and are heavy laden, and I will give you rest. . . . For my yoke is easy, and my burden is light" (Matthew 11:28, 30). He also says that "he knoweth our frame; he remembereth that we are dust" (Psalms 103:14). I realize there are times when circumstances beyond our control make us terribly overburdened and heavy laden and often too busy. When this happens, we have His promise of help and sustaining power (*see* Philippians 4:13; 1 Peter 5:7). We also might have to readjust our priority list and temporarily put ourselves, our health, or our rest near the top. We might have to swallow our pride and admit that we are overburdened or overtired and ask for some help.

* * *

The Great Spirit scooped up the tiny chipmunk and held him cupped in his hand. "Let me down! Let me down!" cried the little chipmunk. "You are interrupting me!"

"Why?" asked the Great Spirit. "What are you in such a hurry about? Stay in my hand."

"Let me down! Let me down! I must mop up all the water from the flood. See, I dip my tail in the water and wring it out, dip it in and wring it out. Hurry up and let me down."

Looking down, the Great Spirit saw the little chipmunk's mate stranded on a little rise, surrounded by the water from a sudden rainstorm, and smiled tenderly at the brave little chipmunk, dipping his tail in and wringing it out, dipping his tail in and wringing it out.

"Here," he said, scooping him up again. "Let me help you." And the Great Spirit blew with his breath and the waters disappeared.

Then the Great Spirit lovingly stroked the little chipmunk before he set him down. And the stroking made stripes down the little chipmunk's back, and he never forgot.

BASED ON AN INDIAN LEGEND

Adjusting and Tuning

My piano often gets out of tune. It gets a lot of abuse, and when it can take it no longer, it begins to sound terrible. After a little re-adjusting, a little tightening here and loosening there by the master, it sounds lovely again.

So it is with my life. Sometimes it seems to get more abuse than at other times. Many different people are trying to get a different tune out of me. The children are banging on

me, someone wants to use me for ministry, someone else
needs to practice on me. The weather can affect me, and
sometimes I am just ignored or not appreciated. I can only
take so much before I begin to get all out of tune and I begin
to sound awful. I have nothing left to give, except notes that
are off-key, and I begin to grate on everyone's nerves. The
basic instrument is all right; it just needs the Master's touch
here and there. Often, my heart is right, but because of one
thing or the other, my attitude is all out of tune.

Recently, because I wanted to serve the Lord and others, I
overextended myself until I wore out. I began to complain. I
began to see everything from a negative point of view. I
murmured, and the notes sounded terrible. No one could
stand to be around me. I desperately needed retuning. The
Master was there all along, just waiting. He tightened up a
bit on my rest time, loosened the tension and pressure of imagined demands, and before long I was myself again.

Sometimes it is my heart that is out of tune, other times it
is my attitude; but more often, it is just the small, everyday,
mundane pressures and demands and irritations that have
gotten me out of whack, and I just need a bit of minor adjusting and minor tuning.

Sometimes it is something as simple as a good night's sleep
that is needed. Someone once said the best bridge between
despair and hope was a good night's sleep.

When I find myself out of tune, it is usually time to reeval-
uate my priority list, time to check through my schedule and
weed out all the unnecessary "urgents" and concentrate instead on the important. This might mean leaving the dusting
for another time and taking advantage of the beautiful spring
day to feed the ducks with my toddler, who will all too soon
be grown and gone. Or, perhaps, simply resting outside in the
sunshine or watching the stars play in the palm branches, or
the moon reflecting in the little lake out front, will do the job.

Sometimes the adjusting needs to take place in my own mind. I may need to realize I do not have to be all that the magazines and television insist I have to be, in order to be fulfilled, happy, and of use to our society. It might mean obtaining some household help, especially while the children are small. I have had nine different girls help me in my home at different times, and each one of them has been a blessing, as well as a real help to me. High-school girls are often looking for part-time jobs, and I have one friend who even hired a young boy who was able and willing to handle the heavier household duties, such as windows and vacuuming.

There is nothing wrong in admitting that we are not bionic women. I have started my children doing chores at a young age. Each one has his or her own responsibility, which is not only good training for them, but indispensable help for me.

The adjusting and tuning might include some better organization, better planning. Someone once said, "To plan time is to have more time." I strive for and pray for a well-ordered day, and usually this has to be done day by day.

I recently met a woman who gives seminars on time management and priorities. She told me the essence of her seminars is, "In the beginning, God." I have found this to be so important and ever so restful in my own life: putting the Lord and His plans first, giving Him my day when I first wake up.

I have a calendar, a schedule, and certain things I think need to be done each day. I then plan my day or my week accordingly. I begin to carry out *my* plans. But often my plans are interrupted or must be changed. Since I try to be organized, which with a large household is almost imperative, if anything is to ever get done, I panic. Things pile up, and I feel the tension of the undone. But, if I have given that day to my heavenly Father and submitted my plans and activities to Him, I relax. I accept by faith that the interruptions, the sick child, the sudden case of the flu, the eleven telephone calls in one morning, were all allowed by Him.

He knows what I have to do. He knows, a lot better than I do, the difference between the urgent and the really important. He understands the frustration of interruptions, and I accept that if I am faithful, He will allow me to accomplish all He wanted me to accomplish, even if my plans often differ from His. I can then relax and really enjoy my busy, hectic day with Him.

I believe that a well-ordered day can be a real testimony to the peace of God. In a well-planned, well-ordered day, we have to plan time to spend with the Lord. I have found that if I don't plan for it, there is never time. Often I drop in bed at night and suddenly realize I have spent very little time with my heavenly Father.

We also have to plan for interruptions and allow time for the unexpected. A woman with many children observed that we tend to make life so complicated that even a quart of spilled milk throws our schedule and our temperaments into chaos. How true this is. I have often become nervous when I thought I had planned my day but then found I have failed to allow for the numerous phone calls, or that unexpected knock at the door, or an unexpected need of one of the children.

We need to plan for fun, for relaxation. I observed recently that we had become so busy we didn't have the time to enjoy one another and have a good laugh. I once read some good advice that Fenelon gave to the Duc de Chevreuse. The Duc had become much too busy and too pressured, so Fenelon told him to observe the wise gardener who was planting young trees. He was carefully placing them with sufficient space between for expansion and growth. Fenelon advised the Duc to allow space between his responsibilities and duties. Our spirits, as well as our bodies and our emotions, need space and leisure in order to expand and grow.

Matthew 8:24 says, "And, behold, there arose a great tempest. . . ." Then in verse 26 we read, ". . . he arose, and rebuked the winds . . . and there was a great calm." We do not have to be overwhelmed by the waves of busyness. Psalms 89:9 says, "Thou rulest the raging of the sea: when the waves thereof arise, thou stillest them."

I pray that I will allow Him to rule the raging waves of busyness, that I will be sensitive to His gentle rebukes and His teaching of what is truly important and of eternal value, and allow Him to flood my hectic life with His peace, His calm, His stillness.

What a triumph to go to bed at night with the assurance and satisfaction that I have done all that my heavenly Father wanted me to do. ". . . for so he giveth his beloved sleep" (Psalms 127:2).

4

Wants and Wishes

There will be less someday
much less,
and there will be more:
less to distract
and amuse;
More, more to adore;
less to burden
and confuse;
More, to undo
the cluttering of centuries,
that we might view
again, That which star
and angels
pointed to;
we shall be poorer
and richer;
stripped—and free:
for always there will be a Gift,
always
a Tree!

RUTH BELL GRAHAM

I HAVE JUST CELEBRATED my thirty-fourth Christmas, and the weariness of wants and wishes is preeminent in my mind and still felt in my aching body and feet. The long lists, the endless shopping, the hours and energy spent in walking up and down crowded aisles, making endless decisions, has left me not only very weary, but perplexed and thoughtful. Not that I begrudge Christmas or giving. I love to give. I love to please and make the desires of those I love come true, but the whole issue of wants and wishes has been brought into focus and has raised some provoking thoughts in my mind. It's been said that if people are unhappy, it may be they are dealing with their wants instead of their needs.

Pick up any magazine, flip on the television, or turn on the radio, and you quickly become conscious of the fact that we are preoccupied with the material. The pressure to purchase things—in order to be happy, healthy, successful, beautiful, and so forth—is overwhelming. This bombardment not only makes us weary, but causes stress, anxiety, and even guilt.

So we wear ourselves out earning the money (or our husbands do), we get worn-out spending the money (often on credit, with money we don't even have), and we are worn-out from trying to balance the budget. We stay worn-out from keeping up with, keeping clean, and keeping in order all that we have acquired.

I am sure we all have an attic or a basement or a garage or a closet that is bulging with "stuff," most of which is the visible evidence of wanting and wishing.

I read recently of a woman who was married to a man who had everything; she wished someone would give him something to pick it all up and put it all away. I realize anew, each time I pick up the umpteen toys or sort through my clothes or carry one more item to my overstuffed garage, that wants and wishes have once again gotten the best of me.

Material things are blessings that are to be used, enjoyed,

appreciated, and shared. But many of us have allowed them to become a burden. The burden of "things" does not necessarily rest only with those who have an abundance of things, but is also felt by the one who lacks these things and wishes he had them or is bothered by those who do have them. George MacDonald said, "If it be things that slay you, what matter whether things you have, or things you have not. It is not the rich only who is under the dominion of things, they too are slaves who, having no money, are unhappy from the lack of it."

All too often I find myself bogged down in concern over things—even burdened by them. Sometimes it is the things I have and am trying to keep up with; sometimes it is things I don't have and wish I did have.

I find myself overly concerned about an item I cannot locate or a book I have loaned that has not been returned or reacting too strongly when a child breaks an object. I'm trying too hard to protect, clean, and care for all the stuff in the house. Sometimes, I find myself too preoccupied with wishing for something I don't have. I then spend time rationalizing, contriving, finagling and even envying. If I don't catch myself, soon discontent sets in, and I fail to enjoy all that I do have. I also find myself burdened for those who don't have as much as I do, and I become frustrated and fall under the burden of guilt. I become concerned with knowing where the fine line between needs and wants is to be drawn, where extravagance and wastefulness begin. What is the right attitude toward "things"? How do I obtain a healthy balance? How can I be faithful and responsible and teach my children the same?

Often I am so concerned about this that I almost envy someone like Mother Teresa of Calcutta, who took a vow of absolute poverty in order to serve the poor, and her Lord, in a more effective way. But the Lord has not asked all of us to serve Him in this way, and so the question of faithfulness and responsibility is one we all have to consider carefully—whether we have much or little—if we are ever to be free and unencumbered by possessions or the concern of them.

Why We Accumulate "Things"

My brother was in the Middle East on several occasions and worked with some Bedouins. He learned how sorry they felt for us Westerners because we were so encumbered and bogged down by "things." This is true of most of us.

Some of us accumulate and collect without even noticing, until we find that we can no longer shove, pull, or push one more thing into our closets, attics, or garages. Not long ago, we moved from Wisconsin to Florida. We decided this would afford an excellent opportunity to sort through and get rid of much of the accumulated stuff. So we held a garage sale, we gave to friends, we gave to the Salvation Army, and we did a good job of sorting through and lightening our load. But, in less than two years, we have reaccumulated all the "stuff" and more, and it seemed to happen all by itself.

Much of what we amass is legitimate and necessary. It is for the well-being, health, and happiness of our family. Depending on the family size and individual circumstances, there will be more or less. Some of what we tend to gather is contrived. If I see the magic words "sale" or "discount" or "final clearance," it is as if a giant magnet is pulling me toward the store. I stand there, hesitating briefly, then I enter, look around, browse, snoop, and admire until I locate a "bargain too good to pass up." I contemplate a moment, rationalize, and give in. Another item, another want or wish is added to my already abundant collection. If the little sign on my desk, which reads, "Anyone who buys what they do not need steals from themselves," is true, then I am in danger of robbing myself blind.

Some of our accumulation just happens, some is just for fun, and much is needful, useful, and necessary. But many accumulate material possessions for other reasons. Some seek security in riches or possessions. They don't even enjoy what they have, because they are so afraid of losing it. They tend to be greedy and hoard what they have. And for these, enough is never achievable.

The Greeks have a story about Midas of Phrygia. He loved money so much that he besought the gods to give him the gift of turning into gold all that he touched. They granted him his desire. He was thrilled. He touched the flowers, and they turned to gold; he touched the tableware, and it turned to gold; he touched his food, and it turned to gold. Then his little girl ran to kiss him, and she, too, turned to gold. He then begged the gods to remove his gift. We, too, can become so enamored of possessions that we destroy all around us, including those we love most.

Sometimes our wanting and wishing stem from the fact that we are seeking acceptance or admiration. We are repeatedly told by the advertisers that in order to be accepted and admired and recognized, we have to wear certain clothes, drive certain cars, live in certain neighborhoods, and so forth. I see many women who are wearing themselves out, obtaining the necessary money in order to purchase the proper ingredients so that they can be accepted and admired and acclaimed and recognized in the community.

> She craved for love
> and sought to satisfy her thirst
> with things. With things
> her life was blessed—
> (or so she thought at first)
> such only brings
> a deeper thirst;

as when a man, adrift at sea,
sun bleached and wind parched, craves
to satisfy his thirst with the salt waves
—only to find his last end even worse;
so, surfeited, unsatisfied—not greed,
but thirst, drove her to gather more
than met her need.
Ignoring Love's "fresh springs,"*
ever more crowded, and yet craving more,
at last she knew that she'd become
a prisoner
of things.

RUTH BELL GRAHAM

*Psalms 87:7 (PRAYER BOOK version)

My husband, Stephan, was once visiting a large church in
the South. Afterward, he was invited to a party where many
wealthy, influential persons had gathered. Among them was a
lovely young couple, the picture of prosperity, happiness,
and success. The pastor of this church later told my husband
this young couple had just lost all they owned, but they had
to keep up the image, because in that society, they would
have lost all acceptance, admiration, and recognition, if it
were known. What a burden!

Others flaunt what they have, seeking attention. Others
give very generously (and very noticeably), in order to gain
acclaim or to help relieve their guilt. In this day, and in our
society—where the young and the rich and the beautiful are
more often awarded and acclaimed—many are ashamed and
even apologetic for the car they drive, the clothing they
wear, or the area in which they live.

I have a friend who recently shared with me the negative
reactions she encounters because she drives an older-model

car and lives in a smaller home than many of her friends. Not long ago, I purchased a secondhand VW bug, for running around in. When the previous owner delivered the car, he told me I should be ashamed to buy such a car and live in such a nice neighborhood—and he was serious! It is a very tiring matter, to be so concerned about all of these material concerns.

The Bible tells us that our thoughts and our hearts will be with those things that we treasure (Luke 12:34). So, of course, if our values, sense of worth, self-esteem, and contentment are dependent on things—whether material, social, educational, or other—pursuing these things will become a way of life for us: an end in itself. We will wear ourselves out, wishing and wanting, always seeking, reaching for, and never finding contentment. We will rationalize and convince ourselves that accomplishing this feat, owning this status symbol, moving to another neighborhood, obtaining a certain degree, landing a particular job, being included in a particular club, or educated in the correct school, will bring us the happiness we seek, the recognition and acceptance that we long for, the self-confidence and self-esteem that is so important to us.

But the Scriptures tell us, especially in Matthew 6 and Luke 12, that we are not to place our confidence in *things*. Our lives "consist not in the abundance of the things that we possess" (*see* Luke 12:15). I find myself becoming entangled in this way of thinking more often than I would like to admit. It is so subtle. It creeps up on me unnoticed, and all of a sudden, I wake up and realize I have fallen for the same lies and tricks that Satan used with Eve in the Garden of Eden.

Discontentment started right in the Garden of Eden. Eve had everything that her heart could possibly desire. God had thought of everything to make her life perfect. She had a perfect environment; all her needs and wants were supplied. She had no cares, no worries, a husband who loved her, and yet Satan was able to successfully tempt her with discontent. Paradise and all that it afforded was not enough; she wanted more.

Aren't many of us just like that? We want more and better and best. The real danger in discontentment lies in the fact that, in always desiring more and never being satisfied with all we have, it isn't long before we are looking longingly at the forbidden. David, too, had all he could possibly want and more, but he became bored and discontented. Then when he was tempted, he did not resist, but took what was forbidden.

Learning Contentment

Bertrand Russell once said, "Doing without things that one wants is an essential part of happiness." Nevertheless, it is quite easy to become discontented when we live in a country where so much is so easily attainable and where so much emphasis is placed on achievements and material possessions. And yet, the Scriptures say, "Let your conversation be without covetousness; and be content with such things as ye have . . ." (Hebrews 13:5).

For many years after we were married, Stephan and I lived in different countries in Europe and the Middle East. For a young American girl, this was an eye-opening and mind-broadening experience. I quickly became aware of the fact that much of what I daily took for granted was sheer luxury, in these countries. We are accustomed to so much that we not only take it all for granted, but we expect it, we think we deserve it, and we often complain if we don't get it.

A friend of mine from England said she was so amazed at how much American women complained. I know I often catch myself not only complaining, but downright grumbling, about grocery shopping, instead of being grateful for our lovely grocery stores, filled to capacity with delicious foods and practical items. How often I have stood in line and heard women complain the lines were too long, the bags too small or too flimsy, the bag boy too slow, and so forth. Often I am ashamed because I tend to take so much for granted and expect so much, and it is not until, for one reason or another, I no longer have it, that I am grateful and thankful for it.

We lived for a year outside Paris, in a big, old house that looked as if it had come right out of a Hawthorne novel. This large, drafty, old house was heated by a coal furnace that we filled and stoked every morning and every night. One day the furnace went out, Stephan was not home, and I just couldn't get it started up again. I suddenly became very appreciative of heat, and a few days later, I wrote:

> Thank You, Father, for allowing me to be cold the other day. We had to bundle up and sit around the little fireplace that wouldn't burn, and we were cold. Thank You, because if we were always warm, we would never know the suffering of those who are always cold. Thank You, because we did have warm clothes to put on and warm food to eat. Thank You for the tea and hot chocolate. Thank You for this little experience. But most of all, Thank You that now we have heat.

Often I don't even notice all that I have, until it is taken away from me. I remember being concerned about all that I had and wondering how the Lord viewed all of this. I questioned my mother about the difference between wants and needs. Where do we draw the line? My husband is Swiss, and for many years, we lived nestled in the beautiful mountains of Switzerland. My mother reminded me of all the beauty God so extravagantly strewed all over that little country—often way up high, where few, if any, venture. The vast, spectacular views; the dozens of varieties of tiny, delicate wild flowers; the rushing streams; the tumbling waterfalls; the quiet, glistening, untouched snow—all of this and so much more is lavished in places so remote that few will ever enjoy their beauty. Yet God, knowing this—knowing there was no necessity—generously, lavishly spread His beauty there. The ". . . living God, who giveth us richly all things to enjoy" (1 Timothy 6:17), is anything but stingy. Our heavenly Father's line between wants and needs is not always clearly defined. His concern is with our heart and with our attitude, more than with our abundance or lack of it.

The Scriptures have little to say about how much or how little we should have. Although the Bible warns of placing our confidence and trust in riches (1 Timothy 6) or our love in money and possessions, it does not condemn wealth, nor does it teach it is wrong to be rich or to possess much of this world's riches. It does remind us often that all things are a gift from God and we brought nothing into this world, so we can take nothing out. Daddy, speaking on this subject, used to ask if anyone had ever seen a hearse pulling a U-haul.

Jesus taught a very balanced, realistic view of money and possessions. He taught those who have little not to worry, and reminded them how He cares for the flowers and the birds. If He cares so bountifully for them, won't He also care for us? He says, " . . . do not be anxious . . . your heavenly Father knows that you need them all" (Matthew 6:31, 32 RSV).

I recently met the most attractive, cheerful woman, whose husband is the pastor of a rather large church. I had been told previously, by mutual friends, that this little lady had come from a nice, southern home of some means and had met and fallen in love with a man who was called into the ministry.

Before they were married, he told her that he felt led of the Lord to always remain totally dependent on his heavenly Father, and that in order for him to do this, he felt he would have to strictly limit his income and trust the Lord to supply all their needs. They have had some interesting moments, to say the least, but over the years, the Lord has always faithfully provided for their every need.

During the course of the evening, this pastor's wife told me that recently she had invited several people to come for Sunday lunch. By Wednesday, her refrigerator was bare, her pocketbook empty, and her bank account depleted. She said nothing to anyone, but she began to pray.

Friday came, and she thought that with guests coming for dinner on Sunday, she should go to the store, but her financial situation remained the same. In the meantime, she and her family were eating rather sparsely.

Saturday arrived with still no money and no food, so she asked the Lord if she should call her guests and cancel. She received a "No. Wait" answer, so continued to pray and to wait. She decided to sit there and watch a miracle happen.

Later Saturday night, the telephone rang. It was someone who told her they had planned a big cookout, but it had been rained out. Could she use some salad and some beans, and so forth? Could she! She thanked them and her heavenly Father. A few minutes later, the phone rang again. It was a member of their church, who had just received two hams and wanted to know if she could use one. Her Sunday dinner was all supplied, the menu planned, and the food all cooked.

Now, of course, the Lord doesn't intend all of us to live like this couple, but it does show how the Lord supplies all our needs, and that He cares about the details of our lives. Those who have everything to live with and little to live for He reminds that all material blessings are temporary, and come from Him; so be grateful, thankful, and generous (Luke 12 and 1 Timothy 6). I read recently that God blesses some with money in order to make them a blessing, not to pamper them.

The Scriptures also teach that we are to be careful not to

become too attached to earthly things: not to set our affection on things of the earth (Colossians 3:2). We are to remember that everything comes from the Lord and belongs to Him. We have the beautiful example of Job, who lost everything and yet was able to say, " . . . the Lord gave, and the Lord hath taken away; blessed be the name of the Lord" (Job 1:21).

I went away to boarding school for my high-school years. My best friend and roommate was a lovely girl from a wealthy family. Her father was a very successful builder on the West Coast, who was a dedicated, delightful Christian. She had everything her heart could wish for. Her mother often sent her large boxes of beautiful clothes, foodstuffs, and money. One summer they generously paid my way to California for a visit. They had a lovely home, which resembled those I had seen in movies or on television. Two large, expensive cars were housed in the garage, and a maid took care of the house. I was treated as I imagined royalty would have been treated. They took me to fine restaurants, to all the lovely, exciting sights, and even purchased beautiful gifts for me. I watched this family and was so impressed; with all their material abundance, they were so completely unspoiled.

A few years later, the father lost everything he had in a bad business deal. Not only did he lose the business, but they had to move from their beautiful home and give up all the luxuries they were so accustomed to. Where they had been used to bestowing generously on others, they now were dependent upon the gifts and generosity of others. Even their car had to be given to them by a friend. Again I watched them, and I did not notice the slightest change. They were just as happy, just as content, just as joyful, just as loving, and just as generous. It was as if their loss had not made the slightest difference to them. Oh, I am sure that there were adjustments, but in their spirit, in their attitude, in their contentment, there was little, if any, change.

They had learned the true meaning of contentment. They had learned what Paul meant when he said:

> . . . I have learned how to be content . . . in whatever state I am. I know how to be abased and live humbly in straitened circumstances, and I know also how to enjoy plenty and live in abundance. I have learned in any and all circumstances, the secret of facing every situation, whether well-fed or going hungry, having a sufficiency and to spare or going without and being in want. I have strength for all things in Christ Who empowers me . . .
>   [I am self-sufficient in Christ's sufficiency].

My roommate's family had found their contentment in Christ, in the love that they had for one another, and in the happy, fun-loving relationships they had formed with one another, so they were able to hold lightly their possessions. I could say the same of them that C. S. Lewis said of George MacDonald: "He appears to have been a sunny, playful man, deeply appreciative of all really beautiful and delicious things that money can buy, and no less deeply content to do without them."

I have never been in a situation where I actually lost or had to give up everything, but the Lord has tested my willingness on more than one occasion. For example, after Stephan and I married, we lived in Europe for about eight years. One summer we came to the United States to visit my family. While we were here, the decision was made to stay, in order for Stephan to continue his education and pursue his desire for a Ph.D. in psychology. We decided it was not worth sending for all of our "stuff," so with the exception of a few favorite items and sentimental objects, we left it all behind and started from scratch. I learned that those things had so little importance. Being together and doing what we believed the Lord wanted us to do was so much more important, so much more meaningful than all the material possessions we had amassed in those eight years.

But, as the years pass and the accumulation of stuff continues, I tend to forget again where real importance and real contentment lies. I am quite sentimental, and I tend to become attached to things. I was reminded of that again recently, when we planned to evacuate our home because of the threat of a hurricane. My first priority was the safety of the children, but I still had a difficult time deciding to leave the house, the "things," the "stuff," the temporary possessions that "moth and rust corrupt." (In our house, it is mice, mildew, children, and dogs.) When I realized my reluctance to leave, I was ashamed and gently rebuked by the Lord and Stephan.

Acknowledging the Source

In Acts, Paul reminds us of Christ's teaching that, ". . . It is more blessed to give than to receive" (Acts 20:35). Generosity and sharing cheerfully is taught throughout the Bible. We are told in Proverbs that, "When you help the poor you are lending to the Lord . . ." (Proverbs 19:17 LB). Also, "If you give to the poor, your needs will be supplied! But a curse upon those who close their eyes to poverty" (Proverbs 28:27 LB). We are also told that "those who [generously] scatter abroad . . . increase more. . . . The liberal person shall be enriched, and he who waters shall himself be watered" (Proverbs 11:24, 25 AMPLIFIED). ". . . a bountiful eye shall be blessed, for he gives of his bread to the poor" (Proverbs 22:9 AMPLIFIED). And Paul tells us in 2 Corinthians 9:7 (AMPLIFIED) that we are to give, ". . . not reluctantly or sorrowfully or under compulsion, for God loves . . . a cheerful (joyous, prompt-to-do-it) giver—whose heart is in his giving." The last verse in that chapter (2 Corinthians 9:15) reads, "Thanks be unto God for his unspeakable gift." He Himself is our example. He freely and richly gives us all things to enjoy. He has not withheld any good thing from us, including His own dear Son, His unspeakable gift.

It is when we realize that all we have comes from Him, and that He has promised to provide for and care for us, and that He Himself has withheld nothing, that we can share without giving it a second thought. Generosity comes easy to those who realize all they have been given by their heavenly Father.

Sharing brings so many blessings. I am sure any who are old enough to remember the TV program "The Millionaire" watched this program while thinking how much fun it would be, to be in the position to surprise people with a very generous gift. A friend of mine was recently entertained in the home of very gracious, generous people. She was picked up in their chauffered car, driven to their lovely home, ushered into a guest suite, and—as if this were not enough—there on her bed was a new, pale blue negligee set. It is certainly not feasible for all of us to show acts of generosity in such a splendid manner, but we can all open our homes to someone who is lonely and put a little more water into the spaghetti sauce. We can all share simple, thoughtful deeds of kindness. "For whosoever shall give you a cup of water to drink in my name, because ye belong to Christ, verily I say unto you, he shall not lose his reward" (Mark 9:41). The little widow of Zarephath experienced this (see 1 Kings 17:8–16). We can share what we have, whether much or little, not forgetting ". . . to do good and to share with others, for with such sacrifices God is pleased" (Hebrews 13:16 NIV). We can never outgive God.

"Oh that men would praise the Lord for his goodness, and for his wonderful works to the children of men! And let them sacrifice the sacrifices of thanksgiving, and declare his works with rejoicing" (Psalms 107:21,22). Our children are very sweet about verbalizing their gratitude. Following a family outing to a movie, bowling, or just a simple supper at McDonald's, they all climb back into our maxivan, and there is a chorus of, "Thank you, Dada. Thank you, Mama." Of course, this brings instant warmth and pleasure to us.

How much more our simple thank-yous to our heavenly Father must bring Him pleasure.

When Jesus healed the ten lepers (Luke 17), and only one returned to thank Him, He was grieved. We are not told in Scripture why the other nine failed to give thanks, but perhaps they simply forgot, or perhaps they thought they deserved what they had received, or perhaps they were too busy telling others about what had happened to stop and give thanks and praise where it was due.

I remember once being so grateful for springtime: the new grass, the small, pale green leaves budding on the willow tree, the warm, balmy breeze, the tiny crocuses pushing their way up through the soil, and the sheer pleasure of once again being out-of-doors after a long winter. I was sharing my pleasure and my gratefulness with my little four-year-old son when, all of a sudden, he turned to me and said, "Mama, thank God, not me."

It is interesting to note in Scripture that the praise sacrifices—those of devotion, provision, and thanksgiving—were voluntary expressions of worship. Our receiving these things is not dependent on our giving of thanks, but oh, how it pleases the Lord when we simply look up and say, "Thank You." I have found that expressing thankfulness and appreciation is often a matter of practice and habit. We need to simply....

> Count your many blessings—
> Name them one by one;
> and it will surprise you
> what the Lord hath done.

> JOHNSON OATMAN, JR.

We do not have to be wearied and burdened by "things," or encumbered by possessions. We do not need to be under the rule and dominion of the social pressure of wants and wishes. What a comfort and relief, to know, as someone has said, that wealth is not found in the abundance of our possessions, but in the fewness of our wants. The Lord not only gives us richly of all things, but He gives us richly all things to enjoy. We can relax and enjoy all that He has given us when we realize that our contentment is in ". . . knowing all is well between us" (Psalms 17:15 LB).

Let us be like George MacDonald, who said, "Let me if I may, be ever welcomed into my room in winter by a glowing hearth, in summer by a vase of flowers; if I may not, let me then think how nice they would be, and bury myself in my work. I do not think the road to contentment lies in despising what we have not got. Let us acknowledge all good, all delight that the world holds, and be content without it."

5

Weights

I traveled down a lonely road,
and no one seemed to care,
the burden on my weary back,
now bowed me to despair.
I oft complained to Jesus
How folks were treating me,
And then, I heard Him say,
so tenderly.
"My feet were also weary
upon the Calvary road,
The cross became so heavy
I fell beneath the load.
So, be faithful weary pilgrim
The morning I can see
Just lift your cross
and follow close to me."

IRA F. STANPHILL

IF YOU WERE TO come to my home for a visit, the very first thing you would see (if the children didn't pounce on you first), would be our grandfather clock. It is not a very fancy clock, or very old, but it is pretty, with a delightful sound, and it is positioned in a most strategic place.

Because of the floor plan of our home, I pass through the entrance hall, right past this clock, dozens of times a day. First thing in the morning, on my way to fix breakfast and get the children off to school, as I do my chores, tidy up the house, carry the bundles of laundry, go to the car to do my errands, answer the doorbell, gather the little ones for their baths at night, and finally, as I head for my room after an exhausting day, I must pass the clock.

I receive pleasure and comfort from the steady ticking and from the faithful chimes that ring every fifteen minutes, but there is something else quite special to me about that clock. You see, each time I pass the clock, it is there to remind me that its weights keep it going.

We live in one of the boating capitals of America, and recently, we began to investigate the possibility of obtaining a small sailboat. We knew nothing about sailing or sailboats, so we decided on a joint venture with a friend who did know something and was willing to teach us.

Sitting on the deck in the warm sun, surrounded by deep blue water, feeling the wind in my face and hearing the chattering of my children all about me, soon persuaded me that sailing was going to be a beautiful experience for our whole family.

As I sat there, listening to my husband and our friend discuss the various and sundry facts of this little boat and the principles of sailing, I became quite interested. In fact, I became intrigued by the fact that much of the value in this particular little craft was the amount of lead it carried in its keel. This weight was very significant, because it was the stabilizing factor for this little boat.

Its builders had made a careful study of just how much weight it could carry. Too much, and it would be sluggish. Its frame, unable to carry the heavy burden placed upon it, would move laboriously through the water. Too little, and the little craft would reel from side to side. It would be unable to keep its necessary depth, and the danger of tipping completely over would become very real. Either too much or too little, and the boat would become unstable and ineffective.

This little boat carries another weight that is also vital: the anchor. If we ever find ourselves in a situation—perhaps in unfamiliar territory, or perhaps all alone out at sea—and we have nothing steady or solid to which we can secure our little boat, we just drop the anchor. The boat may turn and sway. It may pull and tug, rock and toss from side to side, but it will remain safe and secure because of the weight of the keel and the anchor that holds it in place.

These weights are essential, but only a superb, experienced master builder knows just what kind, how much, and where to place the weight. When this has been determined, he then discards all unnecessary weight, and the little ship is ready for effective sailing.

The Value of the Weight

Weights are important not only in clocks and sailboats, but in our lives, as well. But, in order to function effectively, to keep afloat, to keep sailing smoothly, there must be an awareness of the value of the weight, a knowledge of its usefulness, and balance—perfect balance.

The Lord Jesus was aware of, and concerned for, all those He saw who were overburdened and laden down with weights and cares. As He walked the streets of Israel, He noticed the many stooped shoulders, the dark circles under tired eyes, the drawn, joyless faces, and He cried out with empathy, "Come unto me, all ye that labour and are heavy laden, and I will give you rest. Take my yoke upon you, and learn of me; for I am meek and lowly in heart: and ye shall find rest unto your souls. For my yoke is easy, and my burden is light" (Matthew 11:28–30). Here Jesus is offering help to all of us who carry burdens or weights; and which of us is not in need of His help?

Stephan, as a psychologist, is constantly involved with persons who are weighted down, overburdened, and at their wit's end. Some of the loads that these dear people carry are overwhelming.

Often we think of suffering only in terms of physical persecution or physical illness. It is difficult to believe and comprehend all the suffering, heavy burdens, and heavy weights that so many carry—often below the surface, down in the keel, where no one sees but the Lord Jesus. In comparison, my little problems and burdens seem so insignificant. But even if they might seem small by comparison. they can also be very real and very troublesome.

In Ecclesiastes 12:5, Solomon speaks of days when even a grasshopper is a burden. Some days I have been so tired, or under such pressure, or so busy that a little thing like making lunches or taking the dishes out of the dishwasher has been a burden. One morning not long ago, as soon as I opened my eyes, the burden of dailiness hit me. I went to the kitchen, then on to the laundry room, and when I saw that pile of dirty clothes, that did it. The tears began to smart my eyes.

> Lord,
> in these frenzied putterings
> about the house,
> see more!

The dusting,
straightening,
mutterings,
are but the poor
efforts of a heavy heart
to help time pass.
Praying on my knees
I get up-tight;
for hearts and lives
are not the only things
that need to be
put right.
And while I clean,
please,
if tears should fall,
they're settling the dust,
—that's all.
Lord, I will straighten all I can
and You
take over what we mothers
cannot do.

RUTH BELL GRAHAM

Such a small thing (especially when I am blessed to have a washer and dryer). Yet, I had had it. I was overburdened and heavy laden. And I am so very grateful that the Lord Jesus never gave dimensions when He said, "Come to me, *all* of you who are weary and over-burdened . . ." (Matthew 11:28 PHILLIPS, *italics mine*). Nor was size or shape specified when Peter said, "You can throw the whole weight of your anxieties upon him, for you are his personal concern" (1 Peter 5:7 PHILLIPS). God, with the universe on His heart, lovingly listens to our small requests as if they were the only ones. The

Lord Jesus is right there, all the time. He is always available, but it is necessary to acknowledge our need of Him, to take His yoke and learn of Him, in order to make effective and proper use of the various weights in our lives.

All of us are affected by burdens, problems, and weights at one time or another in our lives. Many of us are not only affected by our own weights, but also by the weights and problems of others. Many of the problems that we face are just the normal, humdrum ones of everyday life: the burdens of caring for a home; the mundaneness and frustrations of washing the same sticky fingerprints off the same windows; washing the same dishes three times a day; sweeping and mopping the same floor; washing, folding, and putting away the same clothes; the frustrations of toiling daily to just stay afloat, much less see progress.

Making Progress

I remember the first time we took the little sailboat out into the ocean, turned off the diesel motor, and put up the sails. I thought to myself, "Well, we'll be out here forever. I don't see any movement or progress being made." I couldn't see that we were making any headway. Then I went to sit in the bow, way up in the "pulpit." As I sat there, facing backwards, I could see landmarks we had passed. I noticed the shoreline had changed. In looking back, I saw that progress had been made, and I became encouraged. But I also realized there would one day come a time when we would be farther out and in deeper water. There will be days when there will be no shoreline to observe, no landmarks to follow, and we will have to sail completely by faith.

I remember trying to teach and explain to Aram, my three-year-old, 1 Peter 5:7, "Casting all your care upon him;

for he careth for you." I tried to explain this meant that if we had a problem, we could go to Jesus and talk to Him about it. Then I asked him if he had a problem. He replied that he did not have a problem. I then suggested that perhaps when he had a fight with Tullian (his six-year-old brother), that was a problem.

"Mama," he said, "when I fight with Tullian, that is not a problem. But, when Tullian fights with me, *that's* a problem!"

We all experience days when things just don't go our way. Someone or something makes our day miserable, and our misery becomes a problem. We haven't felt well or haven't slept well for a few nights, or we are just plain worn-out. As George MacDonald puts it, "There is always something to be done and no heart left to do it" kind of days when we tend to confuse physical fatigue with spiritual weakness.

At times, I experience this kind of day. I don't know if time is going faster, or if I am too busy, have too much to do, or exactly what it is.

The other day was such a day. I was tired. I had had houseguests and had spent much time with them. I went out into the yard and found the grass needed mowing. I entered the house, to find the clutter needed straightening and the laundry needed putting away. I opened the refrigerator, and it needed replenishing, plus, dinner needed fixing. The kids needed some encouraging, and Stephan needed some loving. I felt overwhelmed and heavy laden by the mundane, the normal, the everyday burdens and pressures of life. The fatigue, the frustration, and the tension all built up, until "my nerves stretched screaming thin and bare for all the world to see," as my mother put it in one of her poems.

David said, ". . . when my heart is overwhelmed: lead me to the rock that is higher than I" (Psalms 61:2). David knew where to go for strength, when he was completely overwhelmed. In Psalms 86:16 he says, ". . . give thy strength unto thy servant. . . ."

I also went to David's source. I threw myself in His arms, pouring out my heart before Him, asking for His strength to do the very next thing I had to do. Sometimes I need His strength just to pull myself out of bed, to face another day of the usual, commonplace, everyday pressures and burdens.

Isaiah 40:31 reads: "But they that wait upon the Lord shall renew their strength; they shall mount up with wings as eagles; they shall run, and not be weary; and they shall walk, and not faint." The beautiful and encouraging thing about this verse is that the word *renew* literally means "exchange." If we wait upon the Lord, we simply exchange our feeble strength for His. And "His strength is made perfect in our weakness" (*see* 2 Corinthians 12:9). The perfect exchange!

The clue here is waiting on the Lord. Sometimes I become so frantic, so panicked, so busy, I call out for His strength, His help, and I hear Him say, "Wait upon Me." He is never frantic, never in a panic. Neither is He in a hurry. "When he giveth quietness, who then can make trouble? . . ." (Job 34:29). So I ask for His quietness, as well as His strength. When we are in a heap, under the pile, we become problem conscious. But when we exchange our weakness for His strength, we become power conscious.

The story is told of a very anxious, troubled, Christian woman. Those who loved her tried in vain to help her overcome her heavy burden. After suffering for many months, one day she came to breakfast wreathed in smiles. Her loved ones were amazed, and asked her what had changed her so.

She told them she had had a dream that night. She had been walking down a busy highway with many others who were tired and very burdened. Up ahead, she noticed there were repulsive-looking creatures who were dropping little black bundles for these dear, already overburdened folk to pick up.

After awhile, looking up, she saw a Man with a bright and loving face walking through the crowd, comforting the people. When she got closer, she saw that it was her Saviour. She looked up at Him and told Him how tired and terribly over-burdened she was. He smiled sadly and said, "My dear child, I did not give you these heavy loads to carry. They are the devil's burdens. Just drop them right here and refuse to pick them up again, and you will find your path much easier and lighter."

He touched her, and peace and joy flooded her whole being. She threw down her load at His feet, and was about to throw herself also at His feet in joyful thanksgiving, when she awoke and found her cares were gone. From that day on, she was the most cheerful member of the household.

The load
that lay
like lead
lifted;
instead
peace.

The dread
that hung
fog-thick, grey,
faded away;
and with release,
day.

The trial
the same. . .
unsolved
but this:

now
it is
His.

RUTH BELL GRAHAM

Unnecessary Weights

At times, I find myself, like this dear woman, loaded down with unnecessary weight. I go around with stooped shoulders and a sad spirit, sailing very ineffectively and laboriously trying to carry burdens that not only add unnecessary weight, but have been placed in my path by Satan, in order to discourage me and cause defeat in my life. Such things as guilt, regrets, worry, discouragement, envy, jealousy, fear—to name only a few. These can cause us to become despondent and sluggish.

Many are burdened by the weight of guilt concerning something in their past. Guilt is not sinful; only the sin that produces guilt is sinful, because, "If we confess our sins, he is faithful and just to forgive us our sins, and to cleanse us from all unrighteousness" (1 John 1:9). David was burdened by the guilt of sin, until he acknowledged it and confessed it; then he experienced forgiveness and freedom (*see* Psalms 32, a Psalm especially for those who feel guilty).

". . . your sins are forgiven you for his name's sake" (1 John 2:12). "As far as the east is from the west, so far hath he removed our transgressions from us" (Psalms 103:12). He not only forgives our sins, but He then puts them behind Him forever, and Hebrews 8:12 says that He remembers them no more.

The story is told of a little nun who began to have visions of Christ. After several of these experiences, she went to her bishop and told him of these occurrences. He listened to her story, then told her, "Sister, next time you have a vision of Christ, please ask Him what was the worst sin I ever committed."

The little nun left and, for some time, had no more visions. Then one day she returned to the bishop, to say she had had another vision of Christ.

"Well," asked the bishop, "did you ask Him what I told you to ask?"

"Yes," replied the little nun.

"Well, what did Christ say?"

"He said," replied the nun, "that He couldn't remember."

Once we confess our sin, the judicial guilt is removed, once and for all, by the blood of Jesus.

The guilt and the emotional burden the guilt produces will disappear in proportion to our acceptance of the facts that God has forgiven us and that, if He can forgive us, we can forgive ourselves. Then, as someone once said, "We must leave the irreparable past in His hands, and step out into the irresistible future with Him."

> Leave it all quietly to God
> my soul
> the past mistakes
> that left
> the scars.
> All bitterness
> beyond control,
> that mars
> His peace,
> demands its toll.
> Confessed to Him
> . . . and left . . .

it would,
like all things
work together
for my good,
and bring release.
I would be whole.
So
Leave it all quietly to God
my soul.

RUTH BELL GRAHAM

I sometimes carry around the unnecessary weight of a negative attitude. Into this kind of thinking creep such things as envy, ungratefulness, fretting, fear, selfishness. I will wallow around in this pool of negative thinking, becoming more and more miserable and making those around me miserable, also, until all of a sudden, I realize it is Satan who is dropping the little black bundles of negativism, and I quickly ask the Lord to forgive me and to "bring all my thoughts into captivity" (*see* 2 Corinthians 10:5).

A friend of mine was being plagued by troublesome thoughts, and I decided to do a little study from the Bible on thoughts to share with her. I discovered, first of all, that the Lord understands us and our thoughts (*see* Psalms 139:1, 2). He not only understands them, but in the confusion and multitude of our thoughts, His comforts delight us (*see* Psalms 94:19).

We are told in Philippians 4:8 to think of the good things, the true things, the lovely things, the pure and honest things, the positive things. We are encouraged, all throughout Scripture, especially in the Psalms, to think and meditate on all that God is and all that He does, to meditate on His Word and on His works.

In Psalms 77 we read that David complained, and his spirit

was overwhelmed. He even said, ". . . I am so troubled that I cannot speak" (verse 4). He then began to think of the Lord, to remember His works and all His wonders. He remembered the Lord had never forgotten to be gracious. He was sitting in the bow, looking back, and he realized that in spite of everything, progress had been made. The shoreline had changed.

David remembered the past victories. He remembered God's strength and His forgiveness, and soon he was so wrapped up in his thoughts of the Lord that all the heaviness disappeared, and he began to sing the praises of God.

Another little black bundle of unnecessary weight that we often pick up and carry around is that of worry. "Anxious hearts are very heavy . . ." (Proverbs 12:25 LB). Worry or anxiety is so prevalent, and there are many reasons for this. Turn on the television any morning or evening, and you will be bombarded with a pretty grim picture of the world. Even the smaller children are aware of what is going on and ask questions concerning war, missiles, bombs, refugees, concentration camps, and so forth.

My little seven-year-old and four-year-old memorize Scripture verses before I tuck them in bed each night, and it was after one such evening news broadcast that I decided that we would learn Psalms 46:1–3:

> God is our refuge and strength, a very present help in trouble. Therefore will not we fear, though the earth be removed, and though the mountains be carried into the midst of the sea; Though the waters thereof roar and be troubled, though the mountains shake with the swelling thereof.

How comforting these verses have proved to be, even to these little ones. But not only the world news is grim. The local news is filled with all the drugs, sex, and changing

values that our children must face, the violent crime that is so
prevalent in our towns, the strange weather patterns, the
economy, pollution, and so many other things that can cause
us to become anxious and worried. Soaring prices cause anxiety about meeting the bills each month, much less educating
our children and providing for our future. The high divorce
rate causes anxiety. We wonder who will be next.

My mother has a little sign above her desk, which reads:
"Fear not tomorrow. God is already there."

When my two oldest children were small, we lived in
Switzerland. There was a narrow, winding road that led up to
the little mountain village where we lived, and near the entrance to the village there was a very deep ravine, over which
a very high bridge had been built. However, this bridge was
old and somewhat in need of repair, and each time we
crossed it, the children made some comment about being
afraid the bridge would collapse under the weight of the car.

One day, as we approached this particular place, our six-
year-old began to voice his fears. His little sister, who was
four, said, "Tetan, look up, not down. Then you won't be
afraid."

The Lord, who is the same yesterday, today, and forever,
(see Hebrews 13:8) said, through the pen of David, ". . . Fret
not yourself; it tends only to evil" (Psalms 37:8 RSV).

And in Isaiah He says, "Fear thou not; for I am with thee:
be not dismayed; for I am thy God: I will strengthen thee;
yea, I will help thee; yea, I will uphold thee with the right
hand of my righteousness" (Isaiah 41:10).

In the beautiful passage that conveys His infinite care of all
His creation, He says again and again, "Be not anxious" (see
Matthew 6:25-33).

Not long ago, we heard a wonderful, clearly presented sermon on the very subject of cares and worries and how we are
to not be worried or anxious or fretful about anything. It

really blessed me, and as we reached the door of the church, I was still meditating on what had been said. We hadn't even crossed the doorstep before our ten-year-old son began to squabble with his younger brother. I was distressed and a bit embarrassed, so I scolded him and sarcastically said, "Well, I can see that church really helped you!"

To which he replied, with a twinkle in his eye, "Yes, because at least now when I fight, I don't worry about it."

William James, the noted American psychologist, said in his book *Varieties of Religious Experience,* "A paradise of inner tranquility seems to be faith's usual result. Indeed, how can it possibly fail to steady the nerves, to cool the fever, and appease the fret, if one be sensibly conscious that no matter what one's difficulty for the moment may appear to be, one's life as a whole is in the keeping of a power whom one can absolutely trust."

Even though I tend to be a worrier, I know it is wrong. When I worry, I am not trusting. When I worry, I am saying that I don't really believe the Lord can take care of the practical details of my life. Worry means I doubt the promises of God, and when I realize this, I am made thoroughly ashamed of myself.

We often tend to go around burdened by sin that has been, or can be, so easily forgiven, or guilt that is unnecessary, or fears that are unwarranted, or negative thinking that is uncalled for. If we are not heavy laden by the burden of envy or jealousy or pride, perhaps we are burdened down by a complaining spirit, grumpiness, or just plain busyness.

Whatever it is, it is an unnecessary weight that the Lord Jesus never intended for us to carry. In fact, He came to take these very things from us and to give us rest.

There is only one way to do away with these weights, and that is to place them at His feet and by an act of our will, refuse to pick them up again.

Triumphant Burden Bearers

Though most of us tend to lug around some added, unnecessary weight, many of us carry a heavy load that is there through circumstances beyond our control: sudden illness; loneliness; the death of a loved one; a rebellious child; depression; financial hardship; an accident; divorce; an unfaithful, unloving husband; an abnormal child, and so forth.

A friend of mine—who has never had it easy, but who is blessed with a sweet love for the Lord and a deep faith in His goodness—recently discovered her husband was involved in questionable business dealings and with other women. Because of these and other circumstances, she was soon forced to leave her home, uproot her children, and move in with relatives in another city. One day she discovered a lump. She went to the doctor and was told that she had cancer. Chemotherapy was prescribed.

Violent nausea, sleepless nights, and complete hair loss followed these treatments. Soon her children, who were feeling the effects of all these things, began to have problems in school. Never have I ever heard this friend complain. Not only does she not murmur or complain, but she often asks me if there is anything she can do for me, such as take care of my children, cook a meal, or bring a dessert.

How does she do it? She is like the mother of five children, who suddenly lost her husband. "What are you going to do now?" a friend asked.

"Now I shall prove the promises of God," she answered.

My little friend has been proving the promises of God. Instead of lying there fretting during her sleepless nights, she has taken her Bible and drawn from the Living Word of God until the wee hours of the morning, and she is strengthened and refreshed. When she tends to feel sorry for herself, she quickly does some kind deed for someone else. When her pain is difficult to bear, she cries out to Him in faith, knowing that He, who also suffered, understands and has promised not only to be with her, but never to give her more than she can bear (*see* 1 Corinthians 10:13).

> The lonely hours
> Have become for me
> Very precious hours indeed.
> Because
> In reality
> I found that I was not
> alone.
> Jesus gently
> Reminded me
> That
> I was His own.
>
> GIGI TCHIVIDJIAN

It has been noted that triumphant burden bearers do three things by faith, which enable them to rise above their difficult circumstances and impossible situations. By faith, they "read love in God's heart even when His face frowns," as James Renwick put it. By faith, they take a positive attitude of acceptance. They do not waste their time or their energy in useless wonderings and questionings. Nor do they allow resentments to rob them of precious strength. This is not simple resignation, but a positive acceptance that God, for some reason, has allowed this for His glory and to fulfill His plan. As Corrie ten Boom says, "God has no problems, only plans."

Dr. Edward Wilson wrote these words to his wife, just before he died in the deep snows of the antarctic: "I shall simply fall asleep in the snow, don't be unhappy, all is for the best. We are playing a good part in a great scheme arranged by God himself, and all is well."

Triumphant burden bearers use their suffering and convert it into a channel by which God can use them to minister to others.

A pastor friend of ours was watching his eighteen-year-old son play basketball one night, when the boy collapsed. They rushed him to the hospital, but a few mintues after arrival, the doctor told his parents he was gone. No explanation or answer has ever been given, but immediately upon hearing the doctor's words, our friend said, "It's going to be all right, because 'we know that all things work together for good to them that love the Lord' " (*see* Romans 8:28).

A few days later, the doctor came to see the pastor, who was able to lead both the doctor and his wife to the Lord. Since that time, he has taken his loss and turned it into a channel through which the Lord can love many other young men—not only love them, but lead and direct them into ministry and service. To date, over twenty young men are in the Lord's service because this pastor used his experience to minister to others.

Amy Carmichael lay for eighteen years in a bed of pain. It was during that time she wrote the more than ten books that have brought blessing, comfort, and encouragement to so many. In one of these books she wrote:

> Before the winds that blow do cease,
> Teach me to dwell within Thy calm;
> Before the pain has passed in peace
> Give me, My God, to sing a psalm;
> Let me not lose the chance to prove
> The fullness of enabling love.
> O Love of God, do this for me;
> Maintain a constant victory.
>
> AMY CARMICHAEL

Triumphant burden bearers not only find peace in positive acceptance; they find strength in using the difficult experiences to minister to others. Their faith then crowns itself by laying back, relaxed and trustful, in His love. "Trust in the Lord with all thine heart; and lean not unto thine own understanding. In all thy ways acknowledge him, and he shall direct thy paths" (Proverbs 3:5, 6). *Triumphant sufferers have learned to leave it all quietly to God.*

> I lay my "whys"
> before your Cross
> in worship kneeling,
> my mind too numb
> for thought,
> my heart beyond
> all feeling.
>
> And worshiping,
> realize that I
> in knowing You
> don't need a "why."
>
> RUTH BELL GRAHAM

They know that He understands, because He, too, suffered. Even if their suffering is caused by the wrongdoing of others, so was His. Even if there is no explanation, they accept and worship and humbly acknowledge that a sovereign, loving God does not have to answer all of our questions or give a reason for all that He allows or does.

Paul Claudel said, "Christ didn't come to take away all pain and suffering, nor did He come to explain it, but He came so that He might go through it with us."

There is nothing wrong in asking why. But we will not always be given an answer. I do know one thing, however: Triumphant suffering is a wonderful fertilizer and breeding ground for a beautiful character. Some of the most beautiful Christians I know have suffered much.

Just as the lapidary, after careful examination, delivers a sharp, skillful blow to the gem in order to enhance its beauty and increase its value, so the Lord does with us. Or, as the faithful gardener carefully cuts and prunes in order that his garden may be more beautiful, healthy, and productive, so the Lord must at times prune us.

Jill Briscoe was once doing a study on vines and vineyards, so she decided to look up the different reasons for pruning. To her amazement, she found that pruning is necessary to restore a weather-beaten vine, to enhance the beauty of the vine, the health of the vine, to increase the vigor and production in an old vine, to remove weak parts of the vine in order to let the sun shine in on other vines. What a beautiful analogy.

Some of us are weather-beaten, and we need restoring. Some have been Christians for a long time, but need a new sense of vigor and purpose. Some of us need the unnecessary weights that weaken us removed. Some of us need to endure pruning in order for others to find the Son. The pruning is never for punishment, but for strength, beauty, health, and service. He may not always give an explanation. He may not always answer our questions. But His all sufficiency will always be able to meet and take care of our needs.

If for some reason He has appointed you special trials, special burdens, special weights, you can rest assured that, in His heart, He has also reserved you a very special place.

Hudson Taylor once said, "Never mind how great the pressure is, only where the pressure lies. Never let it come between you and the Lord, then the greater the pressure, the more it presses you to His heart."

Often the weight we carry is the anchor for our little frame. It anchors us to the Lord Jesus. It keeps us dependent on Him and His strength. It keeps us secure in the storm.

Paul speaks of such a weight in 2 Corinthians 12, when he

tells of having asked the Lord three times to take away his thorn in the flesh—his heavy, troublesome burden. The Lord denied his request because it was Paul's anchor. It kept him dependent on Christ. The Lord told him, ". . . My grace is sufficient for thee: for my strength is made perfect in weakness . . ." (2 Corinthians 12:9).

Paul answered, ". . . Most gladly therefore will I rather glory in my infirmities, that the power of Christ may rest upon me" (2 Corinthians 12:9).

> If loving hearts were never lonely,
> if all they wish might always be,
> Accepting what they look for only,
> they might be glad,
> but not in thee.
>
> ANNA L. WARING

6
Waiting

We are told
to wait on you.
But, Lord,
there is no time.
My heart implores
upon its knees,
"Hurry
. . . . . . Please."

RUTH BELL GRAHAM

CHRISTMAS ARRIVED, with all the joy, excitement, and anticipation that usually accompanies this happy holiday. Our children had been making endless lists for weeks, and each time I was shown another one, I would reply automatically, "Wait until Christmas."

Finally, all was ready, wrapped, and packed for the trip to North Carolina. The closer we got to the mountains and grandparents, the more excited the voices in the car became. The first glimpse of "home," as we drove up the winding drive, and the warm welcome that awaited us—along with homemade apple pie and a cozy fire—all added to our excitement.

This excitement, and the anticipation of all that was yet to come, built to a crescendo on Christmas Eve, as each child (and adult) hung his or her stocking in front of the large fireplace. My daddy gathered all the children around and called Santa, at the North Pole—just to make sure he had received all the lists and everything was in order—then wished him a good and speedy trip. Just as the children were all being hurried off to bed, Santa's sleigh bells could be heard above the roof. (They were donkey bells hung on the chimney and rung by my younger brother at the appropriate moment.) Needless to say, sleep didn't come easily to the children that night.

Christmas morning arrived, and everyone rushed down to the kitchen, dressed in their Sunday best. By tradition, no one is allowed into the living room until all have gathered and finished eating. The children tried to be patient, as the grown-ups slowly drank their coffee and munched their sweet rolls. Just as the last drop of coffee was being downed, my daddy decided it would be better to read the Christmas story before the stockings, instead of later. Amid sighs, he began to read the beautiful story. Even though the children listened, I am afraid they didn't hear much, that morning.

Then, to make matters worse, my sister decided pictures

should be taken as each child entered the living room, so the children were told to line up and enter one by one. This did it. My eldest son looked up at his grandmother and said, in total disgust and exasperation, "Bethlehem was never as miserable as this!"

Many of us find waiting a very miserable experience.

The Strain of Waiting

How often in life we are told to wait. As far back as I can remember, I was told, "Wait until you grow up," or "Wait until Christmas," or "Wait until you are married," "Wait until you have finished school." Wait, wait, wait.

Wait to purchase the longed-for home; wait longingly for the long overdue letter; wait beside the bed of a sick or dying loved one, or late into the night for the high fever to break and the cool perspiration to appear on the hot forehead. Wait up until the wee hours of the morning for the teenage daughter to return from a party, longing for, yet knowing that sleep will not come until she is safe at home. Wait for the answer to your heart's deepest prayer.

I live in a part of the country where, for several months each year, we live under the threat of large storms and hurricanes. The National Weather Service keeps us well informed from the moment a storm begins to develop, way out in the Atlantic Ocean, and gives us detailed reports of the storm's every movement. Although I am very grateful for this service, it has taught me that waiting can be a very exhausting experience.

Not long ago, a major storm threatened our coast. Preparing for this storm became a priority in our home. We prepared, the best we could, by storing up extra food and supplies, purchasing candles and oil lamps, filling all of the bathtubs with water, and packing suitcases for all ten of us, in case evacuation was necessary. By this time, I was tired, anxious, and nervous, and the rising winds and the constant reports of the devastation this storm was leaving in its wake did little to calm or reassure me. Only hours before the storm was to crash into our area, I found myself waiting—for what, I was not sure—but it was unfamiliar, frightening, and beyond my control. I was scared, myself, and found it hard to reassure my children when I tucked each one into bed that night.

So often in our lives, we find ourselves in situations similar to this. We find ourselves faced with waiting, in situations and circumstances beyond our control. We often become afraid and unsure. Nerves are spent, and tensions build. In our fast-paced, achievement-oriented society, waiting is not something we do graciously. Few of us have been taught or have learned the art of waiting. Waiting often makes us feel helpless, even unused. It is often hard to understand our particular situation, and we feel valuable time is being wasted.

I have often found myself asking why, when I have been faced with circumstances and situations where waiting was the only possible course. This is difficult for me, because I have always thought that being effective for the Lord meant being energetic, active, enthusiastic. And yet, often the Lord has required me to be still, to wait patiently for Him.

I am still in the process of learning that waiting on the Lord and accepting His delays and allowing Him to use them, strengthens me and makes my service to Him more effective. Psalms 37:34 says, "Wait on the Lord, and keep his way, and he shall exalt thee. . . ." He has also promised strength to those who wait on Him: "But they that wait upon the Lord shall renew their strength . . . they shall walk, and not faint" (Isaiah 40:31).

Walking is a slow, steady exercise. It is faithfully putting *one foot in front of the other,* and He has promised strength as we faithfully, steadily walk—just one step at a time—with

Him. I am learning (a bit slowly) that, since it is an exercise (and I don't like exercise; it bores me), it takes discipline and practice and plain getting started.

It also takes patience, especially with myself, because waiting to mature spiritually is very hard for me. But then, slowly, steadily, it develops into a beautiful habit, a delightful way of life. Each step builds strength and encouragement for the next one. So it goes, as we walk, steadily and faithfully, one step after another, hand in hand with our heavenly Father.

Waiting and Building

We are not always shown or given an answer to our *whys* in the Christian walk, and I do not believe that our sovereign, loving God is required to give us an answer or a reason. However, Scripture shows us that waiting is a vital part of our Christian growth and experience.

God has a school of waiting in which, among other things, He teaches us such things as patience, hope, and trust; a place where He often prepares us to serve Him better. Waiting is often the place where our relationship with Him grows to new depths and becomes more intimate. I have found that He often uses waiting in my life just to quiet me down, to bring me to a place where I have to be still, and know that He is God, a place where He tells me, "... Sit still, my daughter, until thou know how the matter will fall ..." (Ruth 3:18). Knowing this has greatly helped me in these times of waiting, because realizing there is a purpose has made waiting a meaningful experience, a growing experience. But, I am still in the process of learning that *how* I wait is very important.

Waiting often carries with it the feeling of total inactivity. I find it hard to believe that waiting on God means sitting in an easy chair, with folded hands. I have known people to do just that. They wait in an attitude of resignation and idleness; or they wait in an attitude of frustration and hopelessness; some even seem to be waiting for the angel Gabriel, himself, before they will budge from that easy chair. How much more wonderful and meaningful—and even strengthening—to wait with anticipation and hope, with patience and assurance, while we lovingly and faithfully carry on with our daily activities and responsibilities.

Sometimes this is just downright hard to do. During times of waiting, often our minds and hearts are preoccupied or burdened or heavy and discouraged. Mrs. Lyndon B. Johnson was quoted as saying, "Sometimes the greatest bravery of all is simply to get up in the morning and go about your business." God knows this, and I have found His strength has been there, each time mine has failed. His greatness and my weakness meet and fit together in such a beautiful way, during times of waiting.

In these times I have found the most strength and help from the Scriptures. I have been encouraged by several examples of waiting that I have found there.

Noah, a man who walked with God, waited for God to work in a special way. He waited actively and in total obedience. He definitely did not sit with folded hands in his tent while he waited. God told him a flood was coming and that he was to build an ark, a place of safety and shelter for himself and his family. Noah believed God and obeyed, but during the years of waiting, building, and preparation, I am sure there must have been times of discouragement and even doubt. The people around him laughed at him, mocked him, and gave him a hard time, but he remained faithful amid this hardship and adversity and continued to walk with God and follow the explicit instructions the Lord gave him concerning the building of the ark.

I am sure there were often other things Noah would have rather spent his time doing, instead of building this shelter right in the middle of the desert, but he obeyed without question and built with the assurance that God had a purpose. When I read this, I am reminded that, as a mother, God is asking much the same thing of me today. Our world is not much better than Noah's, and we can see the storm clouds gathering all around us. The floodwaters of immorality, drugs, perversions, unhappy and broken homes are rising almost daily, and the Lord tells us to build a place of security and shelter for our families.

I once asked my own children what a home was to them, and my four-year-old replied, "A place where we come in out of the rain": a place of shelter, security, warmth, and protection.

I attend a small, interdenominational Bible study each week in my community. Lately, we have been studying prayer, and a couple of weeks ago, we were all asked to write down what we would most like our group to pray for. The number-one request from most of the women there was for their husbands and children—their homes, shelters, arks.

There is a genuine concern among women for their families; in fact, for many dear women, the situation has become desperate. We are so often at a loss as to knowing what to do anymore, and there is so much against us. Building a shelter for our family is no easier today than it was for Noah. I admit that, when I look around me and see the results and hear the statistics, I often become discouraged and even frightened. I ask myself, *How am I going to make it? Why should I escape the deluge?*

There is so much to hinder our building. The world's values are so different, and its worldly, self-centered thinking, its total lack of absolutes, and its tantalizing and accessible escape routes all tend to hinder, and even destroy, our work.

As I read or watch TV, or just look around me, I am frightened to find just how effective the world's brainwashing techniques are.

It is not the most popular thought today, to put your family and its needs first; like Noah, we, too, are ridiculed when we try to build a shelter for them, following the Master Architect's plans. With all this against us, we are still told to build, and whenever the Lord tells us to do something, I have found He somehow provides a way. It is true that the statistics are not favorable, but neither were they for Noah. He was only one man. "But Noah found grace in the eyes of the Lord" (Genesis 6:8). Why? Because he walked with God. This is our only hope, our only assurance: walking daily with the Lord.

The women in our Bible study have begun to do this faithfully and on a regular basis, and each week we have such a blessed time, sharing the results of our regular time with Him. Some share how they talk to Him as they do their household chores, others have found a quiet "closet," others have learned what it means to pray without ceasing as they drive the car pool or wash the floor or rock the sick child. Praying for one another has been a real source of strength and encouragement. Our circumstances and situations are all different, but our hearts' needs are much the same, and we all need to walk with God.

I know when I faithfully spend time with Him, I don't find the difficulties so distracting that I give up, nor do I find the outside influences and activities so tempting that I get my priorities all mixed up. But let me become slack in my time spent with my heavenly Father, and it seems that everything begins to go awry. There are times when I even long to quit building for a little while. I get tired and worn-out, and often my efforts seem so futile. I get tired of fighting the current and being a bit odd and different. I get tired of being a good mother, instead of a popular one. I get tired of always being available and of giving and giving, and often, I simply don't have any more to give.

It is in times like these that I turn to Him. I ask Him to take over, and I prove His promises.

Ever since I was young, I have watched my mother's example, and I have learned much about waiting and building. Her life has been one of much waiting and much giving. She built a place of shelter—her ark—virtually alone, with daddy away so much of the time. The waiting periods were often long and quite difficult. With five very normal children, there must have been moments when she longed to lay down her tools and stop building for a while, just to rest. She shared with me one such experience.

"This is one of those unexplainables. For several days, I'd been bone tired and heavy spirited, easily irritable, negative—just not good company for God, me, or anybody. I excused myself early from the children last night and went to bed. At 4:30 A.M. I awoke and got up briefly, but was still so utterly tired, I lay back down, praying. In half an hour I felt better, so got up and got a cup of coffee. And, as I sat with Him, reading mainly from the Psalms, just thinking of Him, His love, His forgiveness, His understanding, all the tiredness and heaviness went away. By 7:00 A.M. I was refreshed and ready for the day."

And 7:00 A.M. was the hour that mother was needed and had to once again begin to give of herself. She never faltered in the building of her ark, nor did she ever stop giving of herself. When she had nothing left to give, she went to the source of her strength and the supplier of all her needs and was unexplainably replenished. So much so, that we children never saw or knew of her needs. She gave us the sunshine, and gave Jesus all the rest.

Her example has been a challenge for me to follow, and it

continues to encourage me. The source and the supplier of all strength and wisdom and love and patience is the same for us, as we build for our families, as it was for her. ". . . at their wit's end . . . they cry unto the Lord in their trouble, and he bringeth them out . . ." (Psalms 107:27, 28). It is so often when we are at our wit's end that the God who is able, is proved.

Waiting Patiently

From the time I was a child, I was always taught to believe in the promises of God. On several occasions He has given me a specific promise to claim for my own life or situation or circumstance. I remember one such promise, which He gave me several years ago for a particular situation. It was Isaiah 1:19: "If ye be willing and obedient, ye shall eat the good of the land." This particular promise has a condition on my part, so I kept my end of the bargain—or so I thought. I remained willing and was obedient, but it didn't seem to me that the Lord was keeping His end of the deal. So, I often cried and complained, "Why, Lord?" or "But, You promised, Lord." Still, it didn't seem that I was eating the good of the land; in fact, I was just plain miserable. I had to wait. He did keep His promise, but it was on His timetable, not mine. And do you know what? In looking back, the waiting turned into part of the "good of the land."

Abraham also received a promise from God, but he had to wait many long years. He, too, began to doubt. He thought he had kept his end of the bargain. Perhaps he wondered if he had misunderstood the Lord, or if the Lord had forgotten His promise. He must have begun to show signs of his concern. Maybe he became despondent or moody, so Sarah proposed they help God out.

Isn't that just like us? When we see our husbands or one of our children or loved ones sad, we want to help them out. This is quite normal; it is part of our mother instinct to want those we love to be well and happy. But, we must be careful and attentive to the Lord, because sometimes our actions risk interfering with the working of God in their lives. Instead of helping, we weaken them with cheap sympathy and get in God's way.

The other day, my four-year-old was standing right underfoot in the kitchen, while I was busily preparing supper. I asked him to go and play somewhere else. A few moments later, I saw he was still standing there. I told him again to move out of the way. I kept working, and a few minutes later, I bumped into him, right where he had been before. I told him again to get out of my way. When he still didn't budge, I asked him if he was going to move, as I had said.

He looked up at me with a twinkle in his big blue eyes and said, "No, I am not going to play; I am not going to do anything; I am just going to stay here and bother you."

Needless to say, he learned something about discipline that day. But, isn't this often what we do with God? We stand right in the way, when He is trying to work. Perhaps He is trying to answer our prayers—perhaps He is trying to work in the life of our loved one, or in that frustrating circumstance, or in that impossible situation—but there we are, right in His way, bothering Him. Often, He could work so much more effectively if we would just quietly wait out of the way.

Abraham loved the sympathy and suggestion given to him by his wife. As we often do, when things become difficult and we see an easier way out, he rationalized and compromised. He didn't have complete trust in his God. He became impatient, and Ishmael was born. Much heartache and sorrow, much frustration and separation resulted. Abraham learned a hard lesson. Isaiah tells us, "They that wait shall not make haste."

God's concept of time often differs from ours, and we don't always like the waiting that results. I was raised around very prompt people. My grandfather was a medical doctor, among other things, and even with his hectic, varied schedule, he seemed to always be on time. My father tends to be ahead of time. When he says 10:45, he means 10:30. Mother has adjusted to this and is also very prompt, but many a Sunday, we girls were left to fend for ourselves in getting to church, because he would honk once, and was gone. Then, at the age of twelve, I went to a boarding school where being late was simply not allowed.

I then married into an Armenian-European family, which practices more the Oriental concept of time. I suddenly spent much of my time waiting. Not being used to this or understanding it (at the time), I hated every minute of it. I not only hated it, I fought to change it. I convinced myself their way was all wrong and my way was right. I had to learn to adjust. Through the years, I have come to see that my ways and my thinking were not all right, and my husband and I have found a very happy balance.

Going through this also taught me something about adjusting to God's concept of time. I will have to admit, even after all these years, I still don't particularly like the waiting periods in my life. I take heart, though, because I know He cannot, or will not, ever disappoint me. He often uses waiting and delays to test me, but even this turns out to be part of the promised blessing. Waiting on God is never time lost.

Waiting in the Desert

I am sure it was only after quite some time, and perhaps only in retrospect, that Moses saw the blessing in his waiting experience. Forty years is a long time to wait in the desert, and Moses had been brought up as a prince, amid the luxury, the affluence, the intellectual atmosphere, and the stimulating activities of the Egyptian court. Then, all of a sudden, he found himself in the desert, alone with God and his own thoughts. Many of us can identify to a certain extent with the experience of Moses. We, too, often find ourselves in a desert of one kind or another, and adjustments are never easy.

Desert experiences, especially at the time, seem so futile, so unproductive, so dry. We tend to spend much time in morbid introspection, because we wonder what we have done to deserve this or what we are doing that keeps us in this desert. Desert experiences come in all shapes and sizes, from times of physical illness to times of spiritual dryness, from times of utter loneliness to times of utter confusion and exhaustion.

For example, the young mother who has been accustomed to the intellectual stimulation of the college campus or the material benefits and adult conversation of a job or career, suddenly finds herself alone with her vacuum cleaner, her stove, and the walls of her home, surrounded by diapers and dozens of mundane (often undone) chores and stimulated only by small voices concerned about small matters.

> For all these smallnesses
> I thank You, Lord:
>
> small children
> and small needs;
> small meals to cook,
> small talk to heed,
> and a small book
> from which to read
> small stories;

small hurts to heal,
small disappointments, too,
as real
as ours;
small glories
to discover
in bugs,
pebbles,
flowers
When day is through,
my mind is small,
my strength is gone:
and as I gather
each dear one
I pray, "Bless each
for Jesus' sake—
such angels sleeping,
imps awake."

RUTH BELL GRAHAM

In this kind of desert, it is easy to brood, to build up resentments, to become self-centered. We are often tempted to pity ourselves, and we often take out our feelings on those we love the most. This kind of thinking, allowed to continue, builds resentment and tension very quickly.

I have also experienced this let-down feeling on returning home from a few days away. When I am gone, I am usually with stimulating people, who are involved with interesting, often world-encompassing activities. I come home all excited and keyed up, only to face a trip to the grocery store, a pile of dirty clothes, and six stimulated and excited voices, all telling me of the latest incident in their little lives. It is then that I am sharply brought back to the fact that Jesus warns us to be careful not to offend the little ones; He even reminds us to be like little children.

Then, once again, I am reminded that my ministry to Stephan and the children is just as important as the world-encompassing activities of those I have just left. I am revitalized and grateful for those who have the world vision, but I am also deeply humbled by the responsibility and privilege that the Lord has given to me. "When ye have done it unto one of the least of these, ye have done it unto me" (see Matthew 25:40).

Several of my friends, who are now in the middle years, are suddenly finding themselves plopped down right in the middle of a desert again, after many years of nonstop activity, exciting happenings, the commotion and confusion that comes from having a family around. Their families are leaving or gone, and they once again find themselves in a desert.

When we all left home, my mother said she suddenly realized that two-thirds of her life was gone. Now that she was entering a new phase, she asked the Lord to show her what He would have her to do for the remaining one-third. For years she had known beyond a shadow of a doubt what His will had been; to raise us children. Now a new chapter of her life was beginning.

The loss of a husband through death or divorce becomes an unfamiliar and unsure desert experience. There are days and weeks of long, lonely hours, difficult decisions, indescribable loneliness, and an ache in the heart that just doesn't go away. Another friend has shared with me the devastation that came over her when her husband told her that he loved another woman. She faced hours, days, weeks of waiting, hoping, having her hopes smashed again and again. Her frail shoulders were stooped with heartache, responsibility, rejection, and burdens that the Lord never intended for women to bear alone.

The burning bush was with Moses when he thought he was all alone, and that same burning bush is with each one who is waiting in a desert. Moses could have sat under the burning bush for forty years, but instead, he allowed God to use this desert time to prepare him, spiritually and physically, for a unique mission that God had for him.

I believe that God has a unique mission for each one of us. It might not be as the leader of a nation, but as the leader of an individual. God is in our desert with us, and He will use it for His purpose. Sometimes it is just for the purpose of having us more to Himself. He wants us to spend a little more time with Him, or He wants our attention in a special way for a time.

I remember when I was a young, homesick bride with two little babies, in a strange country, with totally unfamiliar people, who spoke a language I did not understand. I had the Lord, and I had Stephen, but I was unsure of my surroundings, unsure of my situation, and totally unsure of myself.

Then, one day, Stephan received his orders for several weeks of military duty. I was alone, scared, cold (it was the middle of winter, and there was no central heat). I had no friends, no telephone, and no car. I would have thought it was the desert, for sure, except there were several feet of snow outside. The days dragged by. I used all of my energy to summon up enough courage to face the cold and the language barrier, in order to buy the necessary groceries. I was just plain miserable.

After a few days in this state of despair, I realized that although I was far away from those I loved, scared to death, and very lonely, I still had the Lord. Wasn't He closer than a brother? I decided to use this time to be with Him more, to become better acquainted with Him and lay back in His love. No sudden change occurred, no immediate miracle. I was still afraid, timid, lonely. In fact, I also became ill with the flu, and I remember how frustrating it was, caring for two small children who couldn't understand that I was sick. The miracle came in looking back, because it is the sweet time of fellowship that I had with the Lord that stands out in that experience, not the misery.

Oh . . .
we are dry.
The grass is brown,
the flowers dwarfed,
the garden droops—
All parched plants are hanging down;
this evening angry clouds
hang low—
the air is still,
no storm winds blow,
and no birds sing;
a pall hangs over
everything.
Then
came the rain:
heavy, silent, brief—
no thunder and no lightning
but, Oh! the relief!

P.S. Lord, I am dry.

RUTH BELL GRAHAM

Both blessings and opportunities abound in desert places. Moses found the burning bush; others, such as Hagar, have found springs of water, to quench thirsty hearts and souls. Jacob, in a lonely situation, found a host of angels on one occasion and received a special blessing, from God Himself, on another. An angel came to Elijah in the desert and encouraged him and even cooked a meal for him. Philip found a man seeking the Saviour.

I found out that I can either spend all of my time fighting the desert or allow God to teach me all that He has for me in it. I can sit idle, and be simply resigned to the waiting, or anticipate all He will do in and through this waiting period. I can allow God to use this time to prepare me, to show me His love, and to get to know Him in a more intimate way. We can be simply resigned to the waiting, or anticipate all that He will do in and through this waiting period.

He is all we need, but we will never fully understand this until He is all we have. This is the greatest lesson I have learned in the school of waiting.

Tragedy Into Glory

Few of us have actually been behind bars or in a prison cell, but many of us have experienced prison. Many of us are prisoners of a relationship or circumstances that we can do nothing about, prisoners of guilt, or prisoners of a bad habit.

Joseph learned to wait in an undeserved prison cell. He had been faithful to the Lord, faithful to his master, and faithful to his job. He was well loved, admired, and trusted, plus, he excelled in all he did. Then he was falsely accused, thrown into prison, and forgotten.

To be forgotten is truly a dreadful experience, and few sorrows can compare with that feeling of being totally alone and totally rejected. I can still feel the awful pain in the pit of my stomach that accompanies being homesick. I was sent away to a boarding school before my thirteenth birthday, and even though it was not exactly a prison, and I had not been totally forgotten or totally rejected, I felt as if I had. We have all gone through times of feeling isolated and all alone, wondering if anyone could possibly understand or empathize with our particular situation or set of circumstances. We even wonder, sometimes, if the Lord understands.

I am sure Joseph must have had doubts or questions, too. But the Scriptures say the Lord was with Joseph. For Joseph, that was enough. Instead of allowing any doubts, questions, or frustrations to dominate him, he served and encouraged those around him, as he waited in his prison cell. Waiting, even in an undeserved prison situation, can be used of God. James 1:3 tells us, ". . . the trying of your faith worketh patience." Sometimes it takes faith—a lot of faith—to believe God has a purpose in our situation and understands our circumstances.

The Bible says we have need of patience, and I know I do. In my life, waiting has gone hand in hand with patience. Patience is a fruit of the Spirit, and fruits have to be grown; they don't just appear overnight. I am often reminded of myself, when I read the little sign that says: "Lord, give me patience, but give it to me *right now.*" I often pray for patience, especially with my six children, and I fail to see that it is through these same six children that the Lord is teaching me patience by giving me countless opportunities to exercise it. I fail to even recognize these opportunities, much less seize and use them. Joseph learned patience, and we can see from his example that the practice of patience builds a strong and beautiful character that is tranquil and unhurried. It learns to be content in any God-given circumstance and even learns to bear much without complaining.

My husband's paternal grandmother was an Armenian woman of prayer and unshakable faith. She spent many years under the most difficult circumstances, trying to build and provide a shelter for her little family. Her husband, her father, and all of the men in her family were killed when Turks massacred the Armenians in the early 1900s. At the age of twenty-one, she was forced to flee, with her two babies, to

Greece. Her faith never faltered. Many years later, while still in a refugee camp, her daughter died of starvation.

Her only son was hundreds of miles away, in Switzerland, separated from her by war. When she was finally reunited with him, she found that he would have nothing to do with her simple faith. She continued to pray, and she watched, as he became more and more entangled with sin and pride. She watched as his marriage crumbled; still she prayed. She saw him rapidly climbing the ladder of success, according to the world's standards. She saw him succeed in every business he became involved with, but become more and more empty and miserable inside. She continued to pray.

For over forty years, this little woman prayed. Today, her son, her daughter-in-law, and all her grandchildren love the Lord. There is a little blue chair in the corner of the living room. No one sits on it. A new slipcover protects the old one, which is streaked and faded with her faithful, prayerful tears. It is there to remind all of us who have been affected by those prayers to never give up hope.

James tells us, "Perseverance must finish its work so that you may be mature and complete, not lacking anything" (James 1:4 NIV). According to Barkley, this means the ability to take a tragedy and turn it into a glory.

David, the psalmist, was one who waited in anticipation and in hope. He learned early to wait. He was still a young, high-spirited lad, caring for his father's sheep, when he was chosen and anointed to be king over Israel. Many long and difficult years of waiting passed, before the crown was placed on his head. David learned much in the school of waiting, and wrote, "Rest in the Lord, and wait patiently for him. . ." (Psalms 37:7). ". . . those that wait upon the Lord, they shall inherit the earth" (Psalms 37:9). "Wait on the Lord: be of good courage, and he shall strengthen thine heart: wait, I say, on the Lord" (Psalms 27:14).

David is spoken of as a man after God's own heart, and I think it must be because he was so open and honest with the Lord.

We don't have to put on some false air of spirituality or conjure up some superhuman effort. We can be open and honest with the Lord and yet still learn to wait patiently for Him with anticipation and hope of the glory that is to come.

I have come to accept (although I have to be gently reminded every so often) that my Creator and heavenly Father knows me better than I know myself. He knows and wants what is best for me and for my life of service to Him. Often what I request is not going to be the best for me or is not going to ultimately bring glory to Him, so He says, "Wait." Isaiah 64:4 (RSV) says, ". . . God . . . works for those who wait for him."

For example, I was sure I wanted to marry the first boy I fell in love with, so I prayed fervently to this end. But my heavenly Father knew (my earthly father knew, also) this was not the best for me. The Lord said, "No. You must wait." I didn't understand fully at the time, but as Isaiah said, He was working for me, and He had just the right man picked out for me, as well as a unique plan for me to meet and fall in love with him. I am very grateful now that He said, "Wait."

There is a beautiful little thought in Isaiah 30:18, 19, which reads, "And therefore will the Lord wait, that he may be gracious unto you. . . he will be very gracious. . . ." These little verses have come to mean very much to me through the years. Because God loves me and wants what is best for me, waiting in faith and trust can never prove disappointing.

At the young age of seventeen, I married and moved to Switzerland. The nesting instinct was very strong, and I wanted to settle immediately into a little home with red geraniums hanging from each window and begin filling it with little children. I prayed longingly for this, but again, the

Lord's plans were quite different. The children came, but no permanent nest.

Not until many years and several children later did He give to our family a nest that was far beyond all we could ask. In looking back, I am so grateful for the waiting years. He taught me so much about trusting Him, so much about how He provides for our every need. I learned so much; I deepened; I matured; it was a rich, growing experience.

Growing is not always pleasant or easy; in fact, sometimes it is quite painful. I am still in the process of learning to wait with patience and the assurance that, even while I am standing "out of the way," He is still active. I'm learning to wait, not in frustration or resignation, but in anticipation of all that He can and will do—not in idleness or hopelessness, but with hope, allowing Him to work in my life and prepare me for whatever He has for me. I often fail and disappoint Him in my attitude toward His appointed waiting times, but I continue to ask Him for a spirit that is sensitive to His Spirit, so I may recognize His working and moving in my life and in the lives of those around me. God may test you with waiting and delays, but remember that you wait with and for One who will never disappoint you. "Therefore will the Lord wait, that he may be gracious unto you . . . he will be very gracious . . ." (Isaiah 30:18, 19).

WAITING

Don't ask why
Don't ask how.
Trust,
Rest,
Love,
Wait,
For now.

GIGI TCHIVIDJIAN

7

Exalted Valleys

I will lift up mine eyes
to the hills;
and when I fly
I will lift up my eyes
to the sky;
it is the same
sure,
certain thing
this quiet lifting up,
remembering. . . .

I leave myself
awhile
to let my thoughts
explore
all He had made
and More;
returning
to my small load
at length,
calm,
reassured:
this
is my strength.

RUTH BELL GRAHAM

THE FIRST TIME I went to Switzerland (in fact, it was the summer I met Stephan), I was a young teenager. I remember how curious I was when the place where we were to stay was described. We were told about the house; the spectacular views; the blue lake, with its many tiny sailboats; the majestic, snow-covered mountains; the window boxes filled with flowers. But the thing that intrigued me most was the fact that we were to be up near the timberline.

Being from the North Carolina Blue Ridge Mountains, I didn't know what a timberline was. Our beautiful mountains are covered with shrubs, trees, and growth of various kinds. How surprised I was to learn there are mountains so high that nothing much grows on them. The Swiss Alps, snowcapped even in summer, are spectacular! They thrill and elate all who are privileged to take in their beauty. But nothing much grows on their high, rugged peaks. A few lovely, rare flowers bloom there, but the majority of the planting, cultivating, pruning, growing, and fruit bearing takes place down in the valleys.

These valleys are fertile and well tilled. The fruit borne is various and plentiful. But the valleys there are often shrouded by low-hanging clouds and fog.

A few years later, when I married Stephan and moved to Switzerland, making the Alps my home, this observation took on a new and more meaningful aspect. I began to see the mountains and valleys in a spiritual context.

As a young bride adjusting to marriage and living in a strange country, away from all that was familiar, I began to experience days of disappointment, discouragement, loneliness, and despair. These experiences were not totally foreign to me; I had had such days before. The difference was that, this time, I felt so alone. For example, Stephan would leave in the morning to go to work, and a feeling of panic would begin to flood over me. The hours seemed like days. I would frantically clean, to keep myself from thinking.

From time to time, I would gather all my courage and walk to the nearest little store, only to be met by a large, smiling woman who would rattle off, in French, what seemed to be a hundred words a minute. I would be so intimidated that it would take a week for me to regain enough courage to try it again. I was even afraid to go out in my garden, for fear of my neighbors, who were watching this young American housewife, to see if she really knew how to care for a home and husband.

Once Stephan invited a young bachelor friend for dinner. After we had finished eating, I noticed this friend was quite interested in what happened next. I proceeded to clear the table and head for the kitchen. Later, he remarked how surprised he had been that I had not made Stephan wash the dishes. He thought all American wives did.

I wanted so much to fit in, to please. I not only wanted Stephan to be proud of me, but his family and friends, as well. I tried so hard, and each time I goofed or made a faux pas (and there were many), I cringed and longed to ". . . fly away, and be at rest" (Psalms 55:6). I would often find myself in Stephan's arms, in a pool of frustrated tears, and in spite of the efforts of a loving, accepting husband to encourage and praise me, I soon became discouraged and totally frustrated.

I felt confined to a life of living in valleys, and I grew weary of trying to climb out of the low-hanging fog of discouragement, loneliness, and despair that seemed to so often hide the mountain peaks.

> The hills on which I need to gaze
> are wrapped in clouds again.
> I lift up streaming eyes in vain
> and feel upon my upturned face
> the streaming rain.
>
> RUTH BELL GRAHAM

I even began to question if the mountains really existed at all. I was trying so hard to climb out of the fog that I failed to recognize the opportunities of fruitfulness in the valleys. But, all this time, my heavenly Gardener was using these early valley times to prepare me, to cultivate me, to prune me, to plant seeds that would one day bring forth fruit.

Isaiah 27:3 soon became one of my favorite verses. By just changing the little word *it* to "her" or "Gigi," it reads, "I the Lord do keep her; I will water her every moment: lest any hurt her, I will keep her night and day."

Springs Into the Valleys

It wasn't too long before I began to realize He was sending springs into the valleys (*see* Psalms 104:10). I would go through an especially difficult time, and looking back, I would see I had experienced a very special time with the Gardener. I slowly began to realize and accept that He was using each and every valley experience to achieve His plan and purpose for me, to bring me closer to Himself, and to bring honor to His name. I discovered He was cultivating me into a fruitful, watered garden and that He was becoming more and more the source of my satisfaction.

I have had many varied mountaintop experiences: times when I have been able to rise above all that would normally cause me to be weary; times of spiritual refreshment; times of real encouragement; times of inner tranquility; times of peace and quiet. I thank the Lord for each and every one of them. But when I look back, I must admit it has been during the difficult days that I have learned to lean on the Lord. It is in these times I have learned to put my trust in Him, that I have found He is all I really need. It is during the difficult days, days when I haven't felt at all like carrying on with the daily running of things, that I have found, in my total dependence upon Him, a sweet communion with Him. It is in times like these that I search my Bible for answers, for encouragement, for comfort.

I remember one chilly, foggy, drizzly day in our little Swiss village, when the children wanted to go for a ride in the *tele cabine* that went straight up behind our chalet to the top of one of the mountain peaks. I agreed. We all bundled into the small cable car, and soon we were suspended high above the ground, moving slowly through the fog. All of a sudden, we broke through the fog, and there—all around us, bathed in the warm sunshine—were the glorious mountains. There are no words to describe this feeling. We stepped out onto the little terrace, sat in the warm, soothing sun, sipping hot chocolate, and tried to capture forever in our memories the splendor of this experience.

All too soon, it was time to go, to return to the fog, the mundane, the frustrations, the difficulties, the dailiness of valley life. We descended slowly, and sure enough, we were once again surrounded by the low-hanging clouds, the mountains once again lost from view. But I knew they were there. I had seen them. They existed. I had been encouraged. I returned to my valley with a renewed spirit, and I couldn't help realizing how much this little experience was similar to my spiritual life.

I might experience several dark, dreary days, when I long to mount up in the little cable car and rise above it all, break out of the fog, see life from a higher perspective. I wish to experience that indescribable feeling of peace, security, power, stability, serenity—all that those mountains represent.

My mother, knowing how I felt, wrote these words for me while on a visit to Switzerland:

> Above the clouds
> thick, boiling, low,
> appear the peaks

she came to know
as Father, Son,
and Holy Ghost;
often when she
sought them most,
they would be hid
in clouds from view.
Distraught by cares
she always knew,
silent, unseen
they still were there,
like God Himself—
unchanged, serene;
knowing this
she gathered strength
for each day's journey—
length by length.

RUTH BELL GRAHAM

Slowly but surely, I began to glimpse the obvious: I do have a way out of the fog, anytime I choose to mount up, to rise above, to see the sun, to look at my valley from a higher perspective. I have a way to receive encouragement, strength, power, and "peace that passeth all understanding" (*see* Philippians 4:7).

Lord, when my soul is weary
and my heart is tired and sore,
and I have that failing feeling
that I can't take anymore;
then let me know the freshening
found in simple, childlike prayer,
when the kneeling soul knows surely
that a listening Lord is there.

RUTH BELL GRAHAM

The greatest source of encouragement I have is that of prayer. Many a time I have been at my wit's end about something, worn-out, or so discouraged that I felt more like giving up than trying one more time. I have fallen on my knees beside my bed, poured out my heart to Him, sometimes without a word, knowing, as Spurgeon said, "Groanings which cannot be uttered are often prayers which cannot be refused."

After a few moments, I am refreshed, rested, encouraged, and strengthened for the next length of the journey.

I have experienced that prayer doesn't so often change the outward circumstances or our situations as much as it does transform the way I look at the circumstances and the situations. Often it is our spirits and our attitudes that need changing.

At one point in the journeys of the children of Israel, they began to circle around a certain mountain. They were going around and around. They continued in this manner for many days, until the Lord came and told them, "Ye have compassed this mountain long enough: turn you northward" (Deuteronomy 2:3). So it often is with me. I circle whatever my particular mountain is—discouragement, disappointment, busyness, worry—and soon the Lord has to come and say, "Gigi, you have been going around in circles over this matter long enough." More often than not, it is in prayer that He speaks to me thus. It is in prayer that I realize my attitude needs to change, my spirit needs to be turned around.

The more time I spend in prayer, the better I begin to know God Himself, and the more I see things from His perspective, from His point of view. This in turn brings the needed transformation in my disposition and in my attitude.

Some years ago, we spent a year living in Israel. Often on the Sabbath afternoons we would take a drive out of the city of Jerusalem and into the hills around. These hills are often barren and rocky, and if you leave the main roads, you quickly find yourself in lonely, hot, dry, forsaken, parched areas where few, if any, venture. As far as the eye can see, there is nothing but sand, rocks, shadows, steep cliffs, deep ravines, and hills, hills, and more hills, with shadows playing eerie games of hide and seek. On one such afternoon, I was gazing out over the row of hills when my eye caught sight of what I thought was something green.

I was curious about this strange growth right in the middle of all this barrenness. Then I was told that, unseen to me, there was a desert stream flowing down the side of that hill, and on both sides of this little stream, there was lush, green growth.

Strength From the Word

Each time I remember this little afternoon outing, I am reminded of the man in Psalms 1:3 who delighted in and meditated upon the teachings of God. It was said of him that he "... shall be like a tree planted by the rivers of water, that bringeth forth his fruit in his season; his leaf also shall not wither; and whatsoever he doeth shall prosper."

Another vital source of encouragement for me has been the Living Word of God. As someone has said, He is the Eternal Contemporary. The Scriptures meet our needs at any given point in our lives. They have been meeting needs ever since God breathed His very own life into them. To meditate on them brings refreshment in the desert, gives strength when weary, quenches our thirst, feeds our hungry souls, and keeps our leaves from withering.

One day I may find I am dry, depleted; I read, "The Lord shall ... satisfy thy soul in drought ... thou shalt be like a watered garden, and like a spring of water, whose waters fail not" (Isaiah 58:11).

I find that I need strength, and I read, "He giveth power to the faint; and to them that have no might he increaseth strength" (Isaiah 40:29).

When I worry about the future and how I am going to make it, I read, "I will go before thee, and make the crooked places straight . . ." (Isaiah 45:2).

When I start to think of myself, I read in Mark 10:45 that He came to minister to others, not to be ministered unto.

When I tend to get fussy, I turn to Proverbs 21:9 (LB) and read, "It is better to live in the corner of the attic than with a crabby woman in a lovely home."

There is a promise, an exhortation, a direction, a comfort, or an encouragement for every situation, for every problem, for every need.

I remember, before my sixth child was born, I all of a sudden developed a fear of the delivery and birth. I was very tired, and the thought of the ninth month, the delivery, and the pain frightened me. I began to pray about this fear and asked the Lord for His comfort and strength.

I began to read my Bible, and this is the verse that I read: ". . . I have made, and I will bear; even I will carry, and will deliver you" (Isaiah 46:4). What a joy to read this promise. I claimed it all during the last month, during the delivery and birth. His promise proved true, His strength sufficient.

Mrs. Jonathan Goforth, a missionary to China, had a large family, including many small children to care for. She was also responsible for much of the mission work. Once, when she was overburdened and finding her strength insufficient, she decided to search the Scriptures, to see if there were any conditions for receiving His strength. She says: "The result of my study was a surprise and joy to me, and later a blessing and help to many to whom I later passed it on, because, every condition laid forth, the very weakest could fulfill."

CONDITIONS FOR RECEIVING STRENGTH

1. Weakness: 2 Corinthians 12:9, 10
2. No Might: Isaiah 40:29
3. Sitting Still: Isaiah 30:7
4. Waiting on God: Isaiah 40:31
5. Quietness: Isaiah 30:15
6. Confidence: Isaiah 30:15
7. Joy in the Lord: Nehemiah 8:10
8. Poor: Isaiah 25:4
9. Needy: Isaiah 25:4
10. Abiding in Christ: Philippians 4:13

Some years ago, we were all sitting around the table, having dinner. I noticed that our eldest seemed a bit down. He had been having a hard time being good, especially in school, and he was discouraged. I tried to encourage him and suggested he try to remember some of the Bible verses he had memorized, which might help and encourage him.

This seemed to get him even more discouraged. He said what he needed was a cap with all the verses he knew written on it, so when he needed it, the appropriate verse would fall down in front of his eyes. To this his sister, two years younger, quickly replied, "Tetan [her nickname for him], you are so bad that you might as well carry your whole Bible around with you."

Of course, we had a long way to go in teaching the art of encouragement, but how pleased we were that these two young children understood something of the important place the Living Word of God was to take in their everyday lives.

A Word of Encouragement

Although the Person of Jesus Christ; the Living, written Word; and the open channels of communication we have with Him in prayer are all we will ever really need, He has, in His love, provided other sources of encouragement—that of others. "Anxious hearts are very heavy but a word of encouragement does wonders!" (Proverbs 12:25 LB.) How often I have been lonely, discouraged, down, or tired, and a word of encouragement or praise has been just what my weary heart needed.

Sometimes, after a hard day of caring for the home and family—when the children have scrapped more than usual, when my schedule has been overloaded, the interruptions so numerous—a day when things were so piled up that I was behind the moment I got up—I retire to my room, ready to flop into bed, and Stephan looks at me tenderly and says simply, "Thank you for all that you do." That makes it all worthwhile and easier to tackle tomorrow. A word of encouragement does wonders.

Recently, I had a bout with the twenty-four-hour flu. During that day, four of my Christian friends called, to see if there was anything they could do for me. One said she was going out to the store. Could she get me anything? Another wanted to know if she could help take care of the children. This encouraged and strengthened me and brought such warmth to my heart. Often a letter or a telephone call comes just when I need it most. I have even had perfect strangers approach me and compliment me. Often it has been when I was feeling lousy. Strangers? Perhaps they have been angels unawares.

My mother told me of a friend of hers who was young and pretty, but prematurely grey. One morning she grabbed the first thing she found in her closet, fixed breakfast, and rushed out the door, to take the children to school. After depositing the children, she pulled up at a red light and sat there, slumped in an exhausted heap. All of a sudden, she heard a loud wolf whistle. Looking up, she saw the face of a big, burly trucker. "Oh, God bless you!" she exclaimed!

Simple deeds of kindness—it doesn't take much, to make us feel better: a word here, a note there, a "Thank you," a "You look so pretty today," or "Boy, you did a nice job!"

Stephan has, as my mother says, "Listening eyes," and he has tried to teach me the art of listening. Just a listening ear can be a real source of encouragement.

Some years ago, Taylor Caldwell wrote a book called *The Listener*. In her book she deals with the lives of several persons who have a need to share, to unload. During the course of the story, one after another of these persons finds himself in a room, opening his heart and life to an unseen listener hidden by blue curtains. After their visit, they go away, relieved and much encouraged. At the end of this book, the curtain is drawn back, and the listener is revealed. Behind the blue curtains is a large portrait of Jesus.

Anyone can be a source of encouragement. This gift is not dependent on age or size or capabilities or education. I am encouraged when my four-year-old brings me a bunch of weeds held tightly in his fist behind his back, or when my two-year-old says, "I want to give you a kiss."

An older person can be a source of encouragement and strength by telling me that she is praying for me. A touch can encourage. Often, in passing, Stephan will give me a pat or take my hand and squeeze it, and I am encouraged. Showing interest in the other one, whether it is a child or a friend, encourages the other one.

On the other hand, we can also so easily discourage. I know I often go to bed at night regretting the things I left unsaid and also regretting some of the things I did say.

Instead of encouraging the children in a job they did, I see the one thing they did not do. Instead of praising them for all the good grades they made, I rebuke them for the one that failed to measure up. Instead of thanking Stephan for all the hard work and long hours he gives in order to provide for us, I remind him of the one phone call he did not make or the one bill he failed to mail or the screens that need repairing. I need and soak up words of encouragement, myself, and yet, I so often fail to encourage.

> A centipede was happy
> until, one day in fun,
> a toad said,
> Pray, which leg goes after which?
> This threw his mind in such a pitch,
> he lay distracted in a ditch
> considering how to run.
>
> AUTHOR UNKNOWN

I am too often like this toad, who majored on minors, until the children or Stephan are left distracted or discouraged. And yet, I have often told the Lord that if I could have any gift I wanted, any ministry I could choose, it would be the gift and ministry of encouragement, the gift of helps.

Jesus' whole attitude was one of encouragement, and whenever I have gone to Him, I have never once left discouraged.

"What a wonderful God we have—he is the Father of our Lord Jesus Christ, the source of every mercy, and the one who so wonderfully comforts and strengthens us in our hardships and trials. And why does he do this? So that when others are troubled, needing our sympathy and encouragement, we can pass on to them this same help and comfort God has given us" (2 Corinthians 1:3, 4 LB).

My heavenly Father has encouraged me through the words of the psalmist, when he wrote, "The Lord will perfect that which concerneth me..." (Psalms 138:8). Every day, through every valley, upon each mountaintop, in each circumstance, He is bringing into perfection all that concerns me. He is working all things out for my good and for His glory.

Often I see no growth or very little progress being made. It is then that I have to accept, by faith, the fact that He has loved me too much to stop now.

The story is told of an old Italian artist who had lost some of his skill. One evening he sat discouraged before a painting he had just completed. He noticed that he had lost some of his touch. The canvas didn't burst with life, as it once did. As he went to bed, he was heard to say, "I have failed, I have failed."

Later, his son, also an artist, came to examine his father's work, and he, too, noticed the lack. Taking the palette and brush, he worked far into the night, adding a little touch here, a smudge there, a little color here, a shadow there. He worked until the picture fulfilled his father's vision.

Morning came, and the father descended into the studio. He stood in utter delight before his perfect canvas and exclaimed, "Why, I have wrought better than I knew!"

One day we, too, will look upon the canvas of our lives, and because of the touch of Jesus here, a smudge, a bit of color, a shadow there, a bit of cultivating and pruning, we, too, will fulfill the Father's vision. Jesus will present us faultless before the Father, and we, too, will be able to exclaim, "Why, I have wrought better than I thought!"

". . . he who began a good work in you will carry it on to completion . . ." (Philippians 1:6 NIV). "The Lord will perfect that which concerneth me . . ." (Psalms 138:8).

Those who experience life in the valleys are always looking for a place of rest. This deep longing must be, and can be, met. But it will never be met, if we look for it in the wrong places: in activity, in things, in efforts, in trying so hard to climb out of the fog, or in other people, even those who are closest to us. Pascal once said, "the heart is a God-shaped vacuum and only God can fill it."

Only the fullness of the love of Jesus can fill our weary hearts. We simply need more of Him. He is the fullness of God, and we are complete in Him (*see* Colossians 2:9, 10). We receive Him in His fullness to the extent that we unreservedly turn ourselves over to Him. As we surrender everything, life becomes so worthwhile.

It has been said that there are plenty to follow our Lord halfway, but not the other half. Identical twins were placed in a church nursery one Sunday. One wandered to the back of the room, while the other stayed toward the front. One of the other children, seeing the one in back, ran to the woman in charge and, with much concern, pointed to the one in front and said, "She left the other half of her back there." Do we allow part of us to grow and leave the other behind?

Jill Briscoe tells the story of the little boy who kept falling out of bed. Finally, his mother asked him why he continued to fall out. He replied, "I guess I stay too close to where I got in." How true this is of us. We come to know the Lord Jesus, but we don't grow. We don't submit to the heavenly Gardener. We don't allow Him to work, to clear the ground, to plant, to cultivate. There is little, if any, growth. Then we sit back and question why we are not bearing fruit. We must abide in Him and in His Word, then lay back, submitted and relaxed in His love, allowing Him to work in us and do that which is well pleasing in His sight (*see* 1 John 3:22).

The heavenly Gardener is still at work in this poor field of mine. There is room for much improvement in my life, but I believe that, by His grace, much has already been done. As I continue to grow in Him, living day by day, year by year in His presence, I have that glorious hope that I will one day ascend into the Hill of the Lord. But, until that glorious day, the land I have to possess is a land of hills and valleys.

His thoughts said, The rocks are far too steep for me.
I cannot climb.

His Father said, With Me as thy Guide, thou canst. I
have not given thee the spirit of fear, but of
power and of love and of discipline. Whence
then this spirit of fear?

His thoughts said, But who shall ascend into the hill of
the Lord or who shall rise up in His holy place?
Shall I ever pass the foothills?

His Father said, Is thine heart set on ascents?

The son answered, O Lord Thou knowest.

And the Father comforted him, Commit thy way—thy
way to the summit—to Thy Lord. Only let thine
heart be set on ascents.

And the Father added, Dear son, I will keep thine heart
set on ascents.

AMY CARMICHAEL

As we progress together, I commend you to the loving care
of the Father, asking that He strengthen you, encourage you,
and fill you with the freshness of His Holy Spirit, so that the
frustrations of weariness can become a fruitful experience.
"... as thy days, so shall thy strength be" (Deuteronomy
33:25). Only He can make every mountain low, the crooked
straight, the rough plain, and every valley exalted.

AND THE GLORY OF THE LORD
SHALL BE REVEALED.